GENEVIEVE TAYLOR

# CHARRED

The complete guide to vegetarian grilling and barbecue

Photography by Jason Ingram

*Hardie Grant*

QUADRILLE

# INTRODUCTION

Welcome to CHARRED, a rather useful collection of easy and colourful grilled vegetable recipes. As a passionate omnivore, my overriding desire with this book was simply to explode the myth that good barbecue has to be all about Man vs. Meat.

Barbecuing as a way of cooking, and indeed as a way of life for some, is on an exponential rise. Cooking over fire at home has never been more popular, and the British competition barbecue scene is flourishing. Running alongside that, the appetite for eating more veg and less meat is huge, as we realise it's better for both our planet and our bodies if we make our diets a little less carnivorous.

Up until now, inventive vegetarian barbecue recipes have failed to hit the mainstream with any great impact and are often limited to corn on the cob and halloumi, perhaps with a little damp coleslaw nestled alongside. Not that there is anything wrong with either, and indeed there are several delicious recipes for both within these pages, but really, grilled sweetcorn plus a rather addictive cheese are just the very cusp of what is possible. Within these pages, I hope to show you that the taste of pretty much any vegetable you can think of can be elevated by a little fire and smoke.

When you cook over a grill or griddle, some sort of magic happens: flavours intensify, surfaces caramelise and edges get irresistibly crisp and charred. Plus, the whole theatre around this way of cooking can only add to the experience. Don't take my word for it; there is plenty of geeky science behind what we all instinctively know – that fire basically makes things taste better. The high heat of the grill or griddle causes intense caramelisation of sugars and also causes the aroma- and flavour-enhancing Maillard reaction. This chemical reaction between amino acids and sugars is definitely not limited to the cooking of meat. Carrots, cauliflower, sweet potatoes, onions, sweetcorn, broccoli, mushrooms and so many others are capable of the Maillard reaction given the right temperatures.

My favourite place to cook is outside, and this is where I head given every opportunity. Freeing myself from the shackles of the kitchen and getting out into the fresh air is irresistible, and besides, who can deny that food tastes better when eaten outside? However, as we all know, the weather can be inclement, and while I enjoy barbecuing all year round it's a rare winter's night that would find me outside in the cold and dark. So with that in mind, as many of these recipes as possible have been designed and tested on a griddle pan on the hob as well as on a barbecue in my garden.

Not all the recipes will work on a griddle pan. For some, particularly those from the Low, Slow and Smoked and the Stuffed and Wrapped chapters, you will need to get outside and get the barbecue lit. Look out for the 🔥 or 🍢 symbol on each recipe to see where it's best cooked. A good, hot oven could also be used for a few of the stuffed vegetables (look for the ⊞ symbol), but you obviously can't add that element of smoke that adds so much in the flavour department.

Conversely, not all these recipes are natural candidates for cooking outside – the more delicate fritters and bean burgers actually benefit from being cooked in a frying pan with a more generous amount of oil – those delicious crisp edges cannot be achieved with heat alone. But there is absolutely nothing to stop you taking your frying pan to the fire and cooking them outside. I do this often, for all the same reasons I like grilling on my barbecue.

So, delve into CHARRED. I hope within its pages you will find much inspiration for broadening your barbecue repertoire. Do find me on social media, ask me questions and share your vegetable-meets-fire creations.

Happy grilling!

@GenevieveEats

# CHARRED PRACTICALITIES: EQUIPMENT AND TECHNIQUES

Cooking on a barbecue requires more intuition than cooking inside on a hob. Various factors will affect success – the fuel you are using, the humidity in the air, how windy it is, to name but a few – so you need to learn to go with the flow a little more and adopt a done-when-it's-done attitude. I often think this is why there has been a huge surge recently in professional chefs embracing live fire cooking. It adds another level of challenge: you need to learn to work with your fire, and to a certain degree there's no technology that can help with that; it just comes with practice and a certain amount of confidence. And barbecue cooking is all the more enjoyable for it.

## Equipment

I like to keep things simple in the cooking department and prefer to operate with the minimum of equipment and gadgetry. However, there are some bits of kit that are invaluable. Here are a few of the things I just wouldn't be without:

### A barbecue

Obviously the number one item you need (although do see griddle pan, overleaf), and you can go gas or you can go charcoal. There is a bit (actually, rather a lot) of snobbery about using gas among the barbecue community, which I can understand to an extent. Certainly gas doesn't give you that all-round elemental fire thing that is the main draw for barbecue fans. However, the simple fact of the matter is you can get great results from gas grilling. As something of a barbecue addict I have both in my garden, tending to veer towards the convenience of the gas grill if it's cold and wet and I just want to cook something super-fast and head back inside to eat it. I much prefer using my charcoal grill – the enjoyment factor is definitely higher and it's my go-to option.

The main thing, whether gas or charcoal, is to get a barbecue with a lid, as you then have the option to use it like an oven – the heat stays in and you cook all round the food rather than just searing the underside.

### The fuel

If you've chosen gas, gas is pretty much gas, but with charcoal there are a few factors to consider. Try to avoid mass-produced charcoal from a garage or supermarket if you can. This often contains chemicals to promote speedy lighting and these can taint your food. Really, with the right technique (see chimney starter, overleaf) there is absolutely no need for any fire-lighting accelerants in your charcoal. I would urge you seek out a good lumpwood charcoal, made in an environmentally friendly way with minimal energy input and from sustainable, ecologically sound sources. Making charcoal is an ancient skill that, if done properly, promotes ecological diversity within woodland habitats, so you can feel good about burning it. Finally, with decent lumpwood charcoal it's fine to add the odd lump now and then during cooking to keep the fire going steadily (if you are smoking over a long period of time, for example). You can't do this with cheaper charcoal or briquettes, as they need to be burned to embers before they get near food.

I either buy my fuel online from the excellent Oxford Charcoal Company, or I pick up bags of artisan charcoal from small local producers when I'm out and about on my travels.

## A chimney starter

This is the simplest and most efficient way to get your charcoal lit, and once you've invested in this cheap bit of kit I guarantee you won't look back. It's a simple metal cylinder with air holes and a grill towards the base, and you just fill it up with charcoal, set it on the grill bars, place a firelighter and a sheet or two of scrunched-up newspaper under the base, and light it. Within 10 minutes or so you'll have a whole heap of hot coals at your disposal. Use heatproof gloves to upend these into your barbecue, distributing them to suit your cooking technique (see direct and indirect grilling, below). You can also use a chimney starter to cook up extra batches of fuel to add to the barbecue if you are doing a long cook; just be sure to set it on a heatproof surface. I use an old flagstone.

## Natural firelighters

Little twisty firelighters made from wood shavings dipped in wax, these contain no chemicals to taint your food and are a pleasure to light. Find them easily in wood-stove shops and online, and even in some supermarkets.

## Long-handled barbecue tongs

Things will get pretty hot, so you need the right tongs to turn your food and move things around.

## Leather gloves or heatproof mitts

I have a set of leather welding gloves that are invaluable for manoeuvring the chimney starter, repositioning the grill and lifting off hot trays of cooked food. Although I do wish they were smaller – there must be lady welders out there who would appreciate gloves that fitted!

## A plancha

Otherwise known as a *chapa* or a hotplate, a plancha is a heavy-duty flat cooking surface. I have one made by Netherton Foundry in Shropshire that is brilliantly sturdy and will last me a lifetime. The heavyweight nature of a plancha means it heats slowly and emits the fire's energy in a steady, even way. Which makes it brilliant for cooking fritters and flatbreads and delicate veg that might fall through the grill bars. A plancha makes amazing pancakes too. And yes, I do occasionally cook pancakes on my barbecue.

## A cheap, thin baking sheet

If you don't have a plancha, you can improvise with an old baking sheet, although it will no doubt warp and twist under the high heat, so grabbing something cheap and cheerful is fine. Occasionally a baking sheet is the better thing for the job; for example, if you want quick, high heat under something that would be a bit wobbly directly on the grill bars, like the lentil-stuffed courgettes on page 118. Or with the stuffed mushrooms on page 98, which have a tendency to ooze cheese that you wouldn't want to lose to the fire.

## A griddle pan

With a griddle pan you will be able to add that barbecue vibe to your food even when the weather outside is miserable, or indeed if you have no space to barbecue. Invest in a heavy-duty cast-iron griddle, ideally with a generous surface area covering two rings on the hob to give you maximum cooking room.

## Kebab skewers

I always recommend using metal skewers. Not only are they reusable forever, they won't catch fire like the bamboo ones are prone to. I know that we are often advised to 'soak bamboo skewers for 30 minutes' to stop them burning. In practice I find this to be completely inadequate. As a bonus, the metal helps conduct heat through to the centre of whatever you are cooking so it cooks more evenly too. You'll find metal ones very cheaply in most supermarkets, particularly during the summer 'barbecue season'.

# Techniques

As I mentioned earlier, much about barbecue cooking is learning 'on the job', and if you do it often you quickly learn what works for you and what doesn't. Here are a few things to think about.

### Heating-up time

With a chimney starter and decent fuel you can get a charcoal barbecue ready to cook on in around 10–15 minutes. Without a chimney starter, it's more like 30 or perhaps even a little more. A gas grill will take around 10 minutes to heat up, which is about the same time as a griddle on the hob. Heating up a plancha from cold will add an additional 10 minutes to heating-up time.

All barbecues will have hot spots and cool spots. This is actually a good thing, as you can move food around to suit its heat requirements. With a gas grill, learn where they are, and with a charcoal grill, learn how to create them (see below).

### Direct and indirect grilling

Simply put, you either grill directly, over the fire, or indirectly, off to the side of the fire, or you can cook on both, which you could call two-zone cooking. You can configure your charcoal arrangement in different ways: a ring around the edge, or a pile in the middle with the edges clear, or (the way I usually do it) a sort of half and half arrangement with coals one side and nothing the other. To achieve this with a gas barbecue you simply leave some of the burners unlit and use that side to cook indirectly. I would always advise you to set up your charcoal barbecue for two-zone cooking – if there is an even layer of coals all over you have no wriggle room to move things away from the fire if they are cooking too quickly.

With a griddle pan, you can achieve something vaguely similar to two-zone cooking by starting veg off on a cold griddle so they begin to soften as it heats up. This is useful for grilling something dense like slices of butternut squash. If your grill spans two rings on the hob, even better – you just don't light one half and the heat will transfer across the griddle in a much more gentle way on the unlit side.

### How hot is too hot?

Vegetables can often take a higher direct heat than meat – there are no collagen fibres to tighten and toughen up, and no particularly critical or safe internal temperatures to worry about. So in that sense they are often easier.

It's good to consider the different cooking requirements of different vegetables, as that will affect whether you choose direct or indirect cooking methods, or indeed opt for a bit of both. So something like delicate asparagus will cook best over a quick, high heat, whereas the dense flesh of parsnips is best given the low and slow treatment. In some cases, like with cauliflower or carrots, the ideal thing is a brief plunge into boiling water to start off the cooking process before finishing off on the grill.

When you want to cook different veg at the same time and in the same place – as on a kebab skewer – try to make all the pieces evenly sized so they all come into contact with the grill. If the veg in question have wildly different cooking needs, like the Moroccan aubergine and tomato kebabs on page 26, you are best off threading and cooking on separate skewers.

### Smoking

For the same reasons as above, you can run the barbecue slightly hotter when you smoke vegetables than you would if you were smoking meat. Temperature is not quite so critical. However, some recipes, like the swede on page 90 or the onions on page 83, are definitely designed to take as long as possible for the best results.

To create smoke for flavour you have three options. The first, using whole wood logs, is great if you are cooking on an open fire, not so great on a barbecue with a lid, as there will be too much smoke and it's all a bit harder to control. The next option, and my preferred one, is little chunks of wood that you can add bit by bit as you go. I would start smoking by adding about three to my fire, then top up with the odd one or two now and then. Thirdly, you can buy bags of smoking chips, which usually say to soak them in water before you use them so they don't burn too fast. I have tried soaking and not soaking and generally prefer the latter, just adding them more frequently. When the chips are wet you get something of a damp and rather acrid smoke, which is not altogether desirable. It's worth noting that the hotter the fire, the less smoke effect you get, and that a more gently burning fire will smoke more.

Once you get into smoking you can experiment with all sorts of different woods to give slightly different flavours. My standard go-to wood for smoking vegetables is little Jenga bricks of oak.

You can smoke on a gas grill – it's not as easy, but it's possible. A few come with tubes you can fill with smoking chips and rest over the burners, or you can put the chips into a tin tray and do the same thing. I wouldn't use chunks of wood on a gas grill.

## Note on equipment

Where I have suggested that you use your frying pan or grill pan on the barbecue (and by all means stick to the hob if you prefer), make sure that it is flameproof and non-stick and does not have plastic or wooden handles.

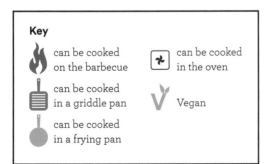

**Key**

🔥 can be cooked on the barbecue

▯ can be cooked in a griddle pan

⬤ can be cooked in a frying pan

✳ can be cooked in the oven

V Vegan

## Ingredient notes

A few final thoughts that are not just relevant to grilling but to all areas of my kitchen . . .

When using spices, try to use whole spices and grind them as you need them – the taste is quite simply a million times better if they are freshly ground. In an ideal world, toast your spices before grinding – it takes seconds in a dry pan over a high heat but adds so much to the flavour.

With spices and herbs I implore you to use them often and to use them generously. To me, there is little point in adding a mini-sprinkle or a quarter teaspoon. Throughout this book you will see me refer to a 'loose handful' of this or a 'heaped teaspoon' of that. Be bold with your flavours and you will be amply rewarded.

When I refer to salt in a recipe, I invariably mean flaky sea salt, unless I specify fine salt. That is my preference, partly because I love the texture between my fingers as I crumble it into a marinade and the crunch between my teeth as I eat. Good salt is certainly worth its salt in my kitchen. I always think if you are cooking from scratch and not eating much processed food, you can be reasonably liberal with salt as a seasoning.

Finally, to olive oil, the starting point of so many of the recipes within these pages. I generally have a fairly standard bottle of extra virgin olive oil that I do much of my cooking with. Nothing fancy, just a blend that will add some flavour but not cost the earth. Then I save the really good olive oil to drizzle over post-cooking when I want a properly good hit of what is undoubtedly one of the best tastes in the world.

# Kebabs

# Black pepper and soy tofu and spring onion

**Firm tofu grills, perhaps surprisingly, really well and it is a very effective 'sponge' for soaking up flavours from a marinade. In these sweet, sticky kebabs, the black pepper adds quite a fiery kick – use a little less if you prefer less heat. These kebabs go really well with the miso aubergine and kale salad on page 152.**

**Makes 6–8 skewers**

Tofu always benefits from pressing to squeeze out excess moisture, making it firmer and less likely to fall off the kebab sticks. It's really easy to do: simply take the blocks and wrap each in a triple layer of kitchen paper, then place on a large plate. Place another flat plate or a wooden chopping board on top, and balance a couple of heavy tins on top to weigh it down. Leave to gently squeeze for an hour or so, or for a few hours in the fridge if you have time.

Mix together the soy sauce, sesame oil, honey, garlic and black pepper in a large bowl. Cut the pressed tofu into 3cm (1¼ inch) cubes and add to the marinade, gently tossing together to mix. Set aside for 30 minutes to an hour.

While the tofu is marinating, fire up your barbecue ready for direct grilling or preheat a griddle pan on the hob. Just before you cook the kebabs, brush the grill lightly with a little vegetable oil to prevent any potential sticking, using a silicon brush or a couple of sheets of scrunched-up kitchen paper.

Thread the tofu on to the skewers, alternating it with the spring onions, taking a little care, as the tofu can be a touch fragile.

Grill the kebabs for 15-20 minutes, turning them a couple of times so they cook evenly. Use a fish slice to ease them off the grill bars before trying to turn them, as they can stick a little.

2 x 396g (14oz) blocks of firm tofu (beancurd)
5 tbsp soy sauce
2 tbsp sesame oil
1 tbsp runny honey
3 cloves of garlic, crushed
2 tbsp black peppercorns, coarsely ground
a bunch of spring onions (scallions), sliced into 3cm (1¼ inch) lengths
a little vegetable oil, for oiling the grill

### You also need
6–8 kebab skewers, preferably metal ones

# Yakitori tofu, pineapple and red pepper

**These sweet and sour kebabs start with a sticky marinade of soy, rice wine and sake that is great as a dipping sauce too, or for drizzling over steamed rice. As with the black pepper tofu recipe on page 16, you need to handle the tofu gently when you skewer it, as it's delicate.**

**Makes 6–8 skewers**

Press the tofu to squeeze out the excess liquid as in the black pepper recipe on page 16.

Once the tofu has finished pressing, put the soy sauce, mirin, sake, ginger, soft brown sugar, garlic and chilli flakes into a small pan and set over a medium heat. Bring to the boil and simmer for about 10–15 minutes, until reduced in volume by about half. Pour half into a mixing bowl and the other half into a little bowl to serve as a dipping sauce.

Add the peppers and pineapple to the sauce in the mixing bowl and toss to coat. Cut the pressed tofu into 4cm (1½ inch) cubes and add to the bowl, stirring gently to coat them in the marinade. Set aside for 1 hour.

While the tofu is marinating, fire up your barbecue ready for direct grilling or preheat a griddle pan on the hob. Just before you cook the kebabs, brush the grill lightly with a little vegetable oil to prevent any potential sticking, using a silicon brush or a couple of sheets of scrunched-up kitchen paper.

Thread the tofu, pineapple and peppers alternately on to the skewers. Grill for about 20 minutes, turning a few times so they cook evenly, basting with any remaining marinade as they cook. Use a fish slice to help release the kebabs from the grill as they can be prone to sticking a little.

Serve immediately, sprinkled with the spring onions and the reserved sauce drizzled over.

2 x 396g (14oz) blocks of firm tofu (beancurd)
100ml (⅓ cup) soy sauce
100ml (⅓ cup) mirin
100ml (⅓ cup) sake
2.5cm (1 inch) piece of fresh root ginger, finely grated
2 tsp soft brown sugar
1 clove of garlic, crushed
1 tsp dried chilli flakes
2 (bell) peppers, cut into 3–4cm (1¼–1½ inch) pieces
½ medium fresh pineapple, cut into 1cm (½ inch) thick pieces about the size of the pepper pieces
a little vegetable oil, for oiling the grill
3 spring onions (scallions), sliced, to garnish

**You also need**
6–8 kebab skewers, preferably metal ones

# Harissa potato, halloumi and asparagus with coriander and lemon oil

Waxy salad potatoes, such as Charlotte, work brilliantly on a barbecue or griddle, but you do need to simmer them until tender before grilling. Here they are skewered up with ever-popular halloumi and asparagus and coated in spicy harissa. I used rose-petal-infused harissa because I love it, but any regular harissa paste will be great too.

**Makes 6–8 skewers**

Bring a pan of lightly salted water to the boil and add the potato halves. Cook until just tender when pierced with the tip of a sharp knife, about 10 minutes, depending on how big they are. Add the asparagus for the final 30 seconds or so, just to blanch it very briefly. Drain the potatoes and asparagus and put back into the pan. Add the halloumi fingers and harissa and stir gently until evenly coated, taking care not to break up the cheese or potatoes. Thread everything alternately on to the skewers and set aside while you heat up the grill.

Heat up your barbecue for direct grilling, or preheat a cast-iron griddle on the hob. Cook the kebabs over a medium-high heat for about 15 minutes, turning once until evenly charred.

While the skewers are cooking, make the coriander and lemon oil by putting everything into a jug and whisking together with a fork, seasoning to taste with a little sugar, salt and pepper.

Once cooked, transfer the kebabs to a plate and drizzle over the coriander and lemon oil.

500g (1lb 2oz) Charlotte (or other salad) potatoes, sliced in half lengthways
1 x 250g (9oz) bunch of asparagus, each stalk cut into 3
2 x 250g (9oz) packs of halloumi, cut into finger-thick wedges
2 tbsp rose harissa paste, or to taste

**For the coriander and lemon oil**
75ml (⅓ cup) extra virgin olive oil
a small bunch of coriander (cilantro), leaves finely chopped (save the stalks for another dish, they are full of flavour)
zest and juice of 1 lemon
½–1 tsp caster sugar, to taste
salt and freshly ground black pepper

**You also need**
6–8 kebab skewers, preferably metal ones

# Tikka-spiced paneer, pepper and red onion with fresh mango relish

Paneer is an Indian cheese with rather similar properties to halloumi – it doesn't melt with heat and is great for threading on to kebab skewers as it's good and firm. Just like halloumi, it can stick a little on grilling, so be sure to lightly oil the hot grill bars before placing the skewers on them. You can also cook these on a hot plancha, which helps with the sticking too.

**Makes 6 skewers**

In a mixing bowl, stir together the yoghurt, tikka paste, garlic and ginger. Season with a little salt and pepper. Gently fold through the paneer and peppers. Peel off the outer two or three layers of each wedge of onion and add those, stirring them to coat in the marinade. Marinate for a good hour at room temperature, or for a few hours in the fridge. Reserve the rest of the onion for the mango relish.

To make the mango relish, finely chop the reserved onion and put it into a bowl with the mango, cherry tomatoes, chillies and mint, stirring to mix. Stir through the caster sugar and lemon juice to taste and set aside for the flavours to mingle.

When you are ready to cook, preheat a barbecue ready for direct grilling, or preheat a cast-iron griddle on the hob. When the barbecue or griddle is hot, lightly oil the cooking surface with a little vegetable oil, using a silicon brush or a scrunched-up bit of kitchen paper.

Thread everything alternately on to the skewers and rest them on the hot, oiled grill or griddle to cook. Cook for around 12–15 minutes, turning a couple of times, until the paneer and vegetables are lightly charred in places.

Sprinkle the skewers with coriander just before serving, and serve with the mango relish and naan bread or chapatis.

150g (¾ cup) full-fat natural yoghurt
3 tbsp tikka paste
2 cloves of garlic, crushed
3cm (1¼ inch) piece of fresh root ginger , finely grated
300g (10½oz) firm paneer, cut into 18 cubes (about 2.5cm/ 1 inch)
1 green (bell) pepper, cut into 18 pieces (about 2.5cm/1 inch)
1 red (bell) pepper, cut into 18 pieces (about 2.5cm/1 inch)
1 red onion, cut into 6 wedges
salt and freshly ground black pepper
a little vegetable oil, for oiling the grill

**For the mango relish**
red onion trimmings from the kebabs (see method)
1 large ripe mango, finely diced (about 500g/1lb 2oz)
a handful of cherry tomatoes, finely diced (about 150g/5oz)
1–2 fresh red chillies, finely chopped
a few sprigs of mint, leaves finely chopped
1 tsp caster sugar
juice of ½–1 lemon, to taste

**To serve**
a handful of coriander (cilantro), chopped
naan bread or chapatis, warmed on the grill (optional)

**You also need**
6 kebab skewers, preferably metal ones

# Jerk-spiced plantain, shallot and halloumi

I often make my own jerk spice paste, as I like the extra flavour and chilli heat you get from mixing it fresh, but you can very easily substitute a ready-blended spice mix. In which case use around 2–3 tablespoons of jerk spice seasoning blended to a paste with olive oil. If you have a plancha, this is an ideal time to use it, as these kebabs can stick a little. If not, never mind, just oil the grill bars or griddle with a little vegetable oil before setting the kebabs on top and be prepared to ease them off with a fish slice. They will still taste fabulous.

**Makes 6–8 kebabs**

To make the jerk spice paste, put the ginger, garlic, chillies and olive oil into a large mixing bowl and stir together. Add the allspice, cinnamon, paprika, thyme, sugar, salt and pepper and stir well to mix.

Add the plantain, halloumi and shallots to the spice paste and gently toss together so everything is evenly coated. Thread everything alternately on to the skewers, setting them on a plate as you go. Ideally, set aside for an hour or so to marinate.

Once you are ready to cook, fire up your barbecue ready for direct grilling or preheat a griddle pan on the hob.

Grill the kebabs for a few minutes each side, until the halloumi is crisp and everything is nicely browned. Sprinkle over the thyme leaves and squeeze over a little lime juice before serving.

2 large ripe plantain, each cut into 9 slices
2 x 250g (9oz) packs of halloumi, each cut into 9 cubes
3 large banana shallots, sliced into 1cm (½ inch) thick rings

### For the jerk spice paste
2.5cm (1 inch) piece of fresh root ginger, finely grated
2 cloves of garlic, crushed
1–2 Scotch bonnet chillies, finely chopped (seeds removed for less heat), to taste
2 tbsp olive oil
1 tbsp ground allspice
1 tbsp ground cinnamon
1 tbsp paprika (unsmoked)
a few sprigs of fresh thyme, leaves picked and chopped
1 tbsp soft brown sugar
salt and freshly ground black pepper

### To serve
a little fresh thyme, leaves picked from stalks
1 lime, cut into wedges

### You also need
6–8 skewers, preferably metal ones

# Moroccan spiced aubergine and tomato with minted yoghurt dressing

**The trick to these spiced skewers is to cook the aubergine and tomato separately, as they have different cooking times. In edible terms, there is little worse than undercooked aubergine – be sure to get them cooking first so they have a head start.**

**Serves 2 (easily doubled)**

Tip the toasted cumin and coriander seeds into a pestle and mortar or a spice mill and roughly grind. Transfer the ground spices to a mixing bowl and add the olive oil, garlic, smoked paprika and cinnamon. Add the lemon juice, along with a little salt and pepper, stirring together to make a paste.

Add the tomatoes and aubergine to the spice paste and toss until evenly coated. Set aside to marinate for an hour or so, or up to 12 hours in the fridge.

While the vegetables are marinating, make the dressing by stirring together the yoghurt, mint and garlic in a small bowl. Season with a little salt and pepper and chill until needed.

When you are ready to cook, fire up the barbecue ready for direct grilling or preheat a griddle pan on the hob.

Thread the aubergine pieces on to four of the skewers, spacing them out so the heat can penetrate the pieces. Lay them on the grill or griddle and cook for around 10 minutes, turning once or twice. Thread the tomatoes on to the last two skewers and lay them alongside the aubergines. Grill for another 10–15 minutes, until both are tender, rotating a few times as they cook.

To serve, slide the cooked vegetables off the skewers on to a bed of couscous. Scatter over a little coriander and top with a generous spoon of the dressing.

1 tbsp cumin seeds, toasted
1 tbsp coriander seeds, toasted
3 tbsp olive oil
2 cloves of garlic, crushed
1 tsp smoked paprika
½ tsp ground cinnamon
juice of 1 lemon
16 cherry tomatoes
1 large aubergine (eggplant),
    about 350g (12oz), cut into
    2–3cm (¾–1¼ inch) cubes
salt and freshly ground black
    pepper

**For the minted yoghurt**
4 tbsp natural yoghurt
2–3 sprigs of mint, leaves picked
    and chopped
1 clove of garlic, crushed

**To serve**
cooked couscous
a little chopped coriander
    (cilantro)

**You also need**
6 kebab skewers, preferably
    metal ones

# Mexican spiced veg with caramelised onion guacamole

The trick to these colourful kebabs is to make sure that your discs of sweetcorn, courgette and red onion are all similar in size, so the skewers form neat 'cylinders' that will both turn and cook evenly. Don't worry about wasting the onion trimmings, they get caramelised to add a delicious crisp topping to the guacamole.

**Makes 6 skewers**

Put the corn, courgette and onion into a large shallow dish, add the cumin, chilli and garlic and drizzle over the olive oil. Season well with salt and pepper and gently toss to coat everything evenly in the marinade. Thread the veg alternately on to skewers and set aside for an hour.

Fire up the barbecue ready for direct grilling, or preheat a cast-iron griddle on the hob.

Thinly slice the red onion trimmings and tip into a frying pan. Drizzle in the olive oil and set on the barbecue away from the fire, or on the hob, and leave to cook gently for 30–40 minutes, until softened and starting to caramelise, stirring regularly. Stir in the sugar and move to a hotter part of the fire, or turn up the heat a little on the hob, and cook for another few minutes, until dark and sticky.

When the onions are halfway through cooking, lay the kebabs directly on the grill bars above the fire, or on the hot griddle if cooking inside. Cook for about 25 minutes, turning occasionally, until the vegetables are tender and nicely charred in places.

While the kebabs are cooking, make the guacamole. Use a fork to mash the avocado flesh with the lime juice until smooth. Stir through the chopped tomatoes, garlic, most of the coriander (reserve a little to garnish the kebabs) and season to taste with salt and pepper. Scoop into a serving bowl.

Once you are ready to serve, spoon the onions on top of the guacamole and sprinkle the reserved coriander over the kebabs.

## For the kebabs

3 corn on the cob, each cut into 2–3cm (¾–1¼ inch) discs
2 fat courgettes (zucchini), each cut into 2–3cm ((¾–1¼ inch) discs
6 medium red onions, 2 x 1cm (½ inch) slices cut from the centre of each, trimmings reserved for the guacamole
1 heaped tbsp cumin seeds, lightly crushed in a pestle and mortar
2 tsp chipotle chilli flakes, or to taste
2 cloves of garlic, finely chopped
3 tbsp olive oil
salt and freshly ground black pepper

## For the caramelised onion guacamole

red onion trimmings (see above)
2 tbsp olive oil
1 tsp brown sugar
2 large ripe avocados
juice of 1 lime
a good handful of cherry tomatoes, finely chopped (about 150g/5oz)
1 clove of garlic, crushed
a small bunch of coriander (cilantro), finely chopped

## You also need

6 kebab skewers, preferably metal ones

# Grilled asparagus and flower sprouts, vegan aïoli

**Vegan aïoli is something of a revelation. It uses a fancy-sounding ingredient called aquafaba, which is simply the liquid you normally drain down the sink when you open a can of chickpeas. It's a rather effective egg replacement, as it behaves in a very similar way, thickening on whisking. Ideally you need a free-standing food mixer for the aïoli, fitted with a whisk attachment. Failing that, an electric whisk and a mixing bowl is a good alternative. If you'd rather make a traditional egg-based mayo, see the recipe on page 86.**

**Serves 4–6**

To make the aïoli, put the aquafaba, garlic, mustard, vinegar and caster sugar into the bowl of the mixer and whisk for a few seconds until completely combined.

Measure both oils into a jug and, with the whisk at high speed, begin to slowly add a few drops of oil, allowing it to combine completely before adding a few drops more. Keep adding the oil slowly until it's all gone. The mixture will be quite thin, then all of a sudden towards the end it will thicken; be patient. Season to taste with salt and pepper and scoop into a bowl. Chill until needed – it will keep in the fridge for up to 7 days.

When you are ready to cook, fire up the barbecue ready for direct grilling or preheat a griddle pan on the hob.

Bring a pan of lightly salted water to the boil. Once boiling, tip in the flower sprouts and blanch for 2 minutes. Drain well, then put into a bowl with the asparagus pieces. Drizzle in the oil and season with a little salt and pepper. Thread on to skewers, and set aside until you are ready to cook – the skewers can be prepared several hours in advance and chilled in the fridge.

Grill the kebabs for around 10 minutes, turning a few times so they char evenly. Serve hot, with a sprinkle of smoked paprika if you like. Serve the aïoli alongside.

2 x 160g (5½oz) bags of flower sprouts (aka kalettes)
2 x 250g (9oz) bunches of asparagus, trimmed and each stem cut into 3
1 tbsp olive oil
a pinch of smoked paprika, to garnish (optional)

**For the vegan aïoli**
3 tbsp aquafaba (the liquid drained from a tin of chickpeas)
2 cloves of garlic, crushed
1 tsp mustard (English or Dijon)
1 tsp white wine vinegar
a pinch of caster sugar
200ml (1⅓ cups) vegetable oil
50ml (⅓ cup) extra virgin olive oil
salt and freshly ground black pepper

**You also need**
about 8 kebab skewers, preferably metal ones

# Sticky tempeh and courgette, wasabi dipping sauce

Tempeh is a cultured and pressed soy bean cake from Indonesia that can be marinated and threaded on to skewers in a similar way to tofu. Like tofu, it is a real sponge for soaking up flavours but it has much more texture, a little like crushed chestnuts, and for that reason I often prefer it. It is becoming much more common to find – try Asian food shops or online. I have even spotted it in my local supermarket.

**Makes 6–8 skewers**

Make a marinade by whisking the soy, honey, lime zest and garlic in a mixing bowl, seasoning with a good grind of black pepper. Add the tempeh cubes and courgette pieces and toss well together until everything is evenly coated. Set aside to marinate for at least an hour; longer in the fridge would be fine.

Meanwhile, make the dipping sauce by putting the wasabi paste, lime juice, soy sauce and honey into a bowl and whisking together to form a smooth sauce. Start with the quantities given and add a little more wasabi, honey or soy to taste – you want a good balance of punchy heat, sourness, saltiness and sweetness.

When you are ready to cook, fire up your barbecue ready for direct grilling, or preheat a cast-iron griddle pan on the hob. When the barbecue or griddle is hot, lightly oil the cooking surface with a little vegetable oil, using a silicon brush or a scrunched-up bit of kitchen paper.

Thread the tempeh and courgettes on to the skewers and lay them on the grill, cooking them for about 12–15 minutes, turning a few times to make sure they are cooking evenly.

Serve while hot, with the dipping sauce alongside.

4 tbsp soy sauce
2 tbsp runny honey
zest of 2 limes
2 cloves of garlic, crushed
2 x 200g (7oz) blocks of tempeh, each cut into 9 equal pieces
2 small courgettes (zucchini), cut in half lengthways, then chopped into similar-sized pieces to the tempeh
freshly ground black pepper
a little vegetable oil, for oiling the grill or griddle

**For the wasabi dipping sauce**
1 tbsp wasabi paste, or to taste
juice of 2 limes
3 tbsp soy sauce, or to taste
1 tbsp honey, or to taste

**You also need**
6–8 kebab skewers, preferably metal ones

# Broccoli and squash with Gruyère sauce and toast

**Inspired by fondue, this intensely cheesy sauce is perfect comfort food for a cold wet night. The kebabs and toast both cook brilliantly on a griddle on the hob, so you don't even need to think about heading out to the barbecue.**

**Makes 6 skewers, serving 2 generously**

For the sauce, put the butter and garlic in a small heavy-based pan over a medium heat on the hob. Once the butter has melted, stir through the flour to form a roux. Pour in the wine, whisking constantly until it has formed a thick paste then gradually pour in the milk, whisking all the time to beat out any lumps as it comes up to the boil. Add the nutmeg and bay leaf, then reduce the heat and simmer steadily for 5 minutes. Turn off the heat, add the Gruyère and Parmesan and season with a little salt and pepper. Set to one side while you make the kebabs.

Preheat a griddle on the hob, or fire up the barbecue ready for direct grilling if you prefer.

Bring a large pan of lightly salted water to the boil and drop in the diced squash, blanching it for 4 minutes. Add the broccoli and blanch for just for 1 more minute, then drain well. Tip back into the pan and drizzle in a couple of tablespoons of oil. Add the chilli flakes, if using, plus a good grind of salt and pepper, and stir gently to coat. Thread on to skewers, alternating the squash and broccoli pieces.

Lay the kebabs on the griddle, or on the barbecue, and cook for about 10–12 minutes, turning them over a couple of times until lightly charred. Transfer to a serving plate and cover with foil to keep warm.

Brush the last tablespoon of oil over both sides of the bread and sprinkle on the herbs, along with a little salt and pepper. Lay the bread on the hot griddle and toast on both sides, pressing down as it cooks so you get plenty of handsome griddle lines.

While the toast is cooking, warm the sauce over a low heat on the hob. To serve, pour the hot sauce into a bowl. Serve the kebabs and toast alongside, ready for dunking in the sauce as you eat.

## For the Gruyère sauce

35g (1¼oz) butter
1 clove of garlic, crushed
35g (¼ cup) plain (all-purpose) flour
75ml (⅓ cup) dry white wine
300ml (1¼ cups) milk
a little freshly grated nutmeg
1 bay leaf
150g (5oz) mature Gruyère, grated
25g (1oz) freshly grated Parmesan
salt and freshly ground black pepper

## For the kebabs and toast

400g (14oz) butternut squash, peeled and cut into pieces of similar size to the broccoli
1 medium head of broccoli, cut into bite-sized florets
3 tbsp olive oil
1 tsp chilli flakes (optional)
4 large slices of sourdough bread
1 tsp dried mixed herbs

# Barbecue sauce glazed cauliflower

Hot, sweet and smoky, these barbecue sauce glazed skewers are quite simply the business, and once you have made the sauce, the skewers themselves are a complete doddle. The sauce recipe makes a couple of jars – it's not worth making less really – and is great used on pretty much anything you fancy grilling. The trick with using a sugar-rich glaze like this is to wait until your skewers – vegetables, halloumi or whatever – are nearly cooked through, then brush on the glaze over a high heat at the end of cooking to finish them off. The addition of polenta to the cauliflower may seem a touch odd, but it adds a very welcome crunch.

**Serves 4–6**

Begin by making the barbecue sauce. Pour the oil into a small heavy-based pan and set over a medium-low heat. Add the onion and cook gently, stirring occasionally, for a good 20 minutes, until it is really soft but not really coloured.

Once the onion is cooked, stir in the garlic and cook for a further couple of minutes. Add the remaining ingredients one after the other and bring to a simmer, stirring well as the mixture heats. Reduce the heat to a minimum and allow the sauce to gently bubble away over a very low heat for 30 minutes.

While the sauce is cooking, sterilise two standard jam jars, plus lids. Preheat the oven to 100°C fan/225°F. Wash the jars and lids in warm soapy water and rinse under clean running water. Place upside down on a baking tray and slide into the oven to heat for 20 minutes, or until completely dry.

When the sauce has finished cooking, pour it into a blender and whizz until completely smooth. Spoon into the clean jars and seal tightly. You can also use a stick blender in the pan – just be careful of hot splatters! Store in the fridge, where it will keep happily for 6 months or more.

Once you are ready to cook your skewers, fire up the barbecue ready for direct grilling, or heat up a cast iron griddle on the hob.

1 large cauliflower, broken
   into florets
1 tbsp olive oil
3 tbsp instant polenta (cornmeal)
3 tbsp barbecue sauce
   (see below)
salt and freshly ground black
   pepper

**For the barbecue sauce
(makes 2 standard jam jars)**
1 tbsp vegetable oil
1 onion, finely chopped
3 cloves of garlic, chopped
300g (10½oz) tomato ketchup
100ml (⅓ cup) cider vinegar
100g (⅓ cup) black treacle
3 tbsp brown sugar
3 tbsp Worcestershire sauce
3 tbsp English mustard
1 tbsp hot smoked paprika
1 tsp salt

**You also need**
6 kebab skewers, preferably
   metal ones

Bring a large pan of lightly salted water up to the boil and, once boiling, tip in the cauliflower florets. Blanch for 5 minutes, until just starting to soften a little but still firm. Drain well, then allow to steam dry in the pan for a minute or so. Add the olive oil, polenta and a little salt and pepper and gently toss to mix.

Carefully poke the cauliflower florets on to the skewers, threading them so the kebab stick goes sideways through the stem for maximum integrity. Lay on the grill and cook for a few minutes, until just starting to colour a little on the underside. Turn them over and use a silicon brush to paint some barbecue sauce on to the top side, taking a little time to work the sauce into the crevices of the florets. Cook for another few minutes, then turn carefully with tongs and paint with more sauce. Keep turning and painting until the kebabs are glazed all over and crisp in places. They should take about 10–12 minutes to cook.

# Burgers and fritters

# TWO BEAN BURGERS

Both these bean burger recipes contain a charred vegetable element that I cook either on a cast-iron griddle on the hob or on the barbecue if I happen to have it lit. The burgers themselves are best cooked in a frying pan, as you want enough oil under them to crisp them up, so they are something I either cook on the hob inside, or I set the frying pan on the barbecue if it's lit. Incidentally, both these bean burgers freeze really well once made and shaped. Allow to defrost fully before cooking.

## Mexican black bean burger, avocado, chipotle sour cream

Chipotle chilli is one of my favourite spices, providing not only a lovely hit of heat but bags of smoky flavour too. Grilling the squash adds all-important caramelisation and also dries the flesh out a little so your burgers are not too wet and liable to collapse in the pan.

**Makes 4**

Begin by grilling the squash. Preheat a griddle pan on the hob until hot, or if you have a barbecue going, use that to grill the squash. Using about a tablespoon of olive oil, lightly brush the squash slices all over and season with salt and pepper. Lay on the grill and cook on both sides until tender and lightly charred – about 20 minutes, depending on the heat you give them. Remove from the heat and chop finely, then put into a bowl and set aside to cool down. The cooked squash will keep in the fridge for a few days if you want to get ahead with the grilling stage.

Once you are ready to make the burgers, put the cumin seeds and chilli flakes into a dry frying pan and set over a medium heat to toast for a minute or so. As soon as you smell their aroma wafting up from the pan, tip them into a pestle and mortar and roughly grind.

300g (10½oz) peeled butternut squash, cut into 1cm (½ inch) slices
3 tbsp olive oil
2 tsp cumin seeds
1–2 tsp chilli flakes, ideally chipotle
1 onion, finely chopped
2 cloves of garlic, crushed
2 x 400g (14oz) cans of black beans, drained and rinsed
a large handful of coriander (cilantro), chopped
2 tbsp plain (all-purpose) flour
2 eggs, lightly beaten
125g (2 cups) fresh breadcrumbs
salt and freshly ground black pepper
a little vegetable oil, for shallow frying

Pour the remaining olive oil into the frying pan, set over a low heat and add the onion and season generously with salt and pepper. Cook for a good 15–20 minutes, until soft and lightly caramelised. Add the garlic and stir-fry for another minute, then tip in the black beans, squash and spices and use a potato masher to break the mix up to a coarse purée. Stir through the coriander, then scoop the bean mixture into a shallow bowl. Set aside to cool, then chill for an hour to firm up.

While the bean mix is chilling, make the dressing by stirring together the sour cream with the garlic and chipotle chilli in a small bowl. Set aside.

Put the flour, eggs and breadcrumbs into three separate bowls, ready to coat the burgers.

Shape the chilled bean mix into 4 even-sized balls, then flatten each one to a disc about 1.5cm (¾ inch) thick. Take one burger and dip it in the flour to coat evenly all over. Then dip into the egg, followed by the breadcrumbs, carefully turning the burger over to get an even coating. Set on a plate and repeat with the others.

Pour a thin layer of vegetable oil into a large frying pan and set over a high heat. Once the oil is really hot, add the burgers. Cook for a few minutes on each side, until they are deep golden brown and crisp. Use a spatula to splash a little oil up the sides of the burgers as they are cooking, to help crisp up the edges.

To serve, place a little lettuce and a burger on the base of each bun and top with a few slices of avocado. Add a good dollop of chipotle sour cream dressing, top with the bun lid and tuck in.

**For the chipotle sour cream**
3 tbsp sour cream
1 clove of garlic, crushed
½ tsp chipotle chilli flakes

**To serve**
a few lettuce leaves
4 burger buns, lightly toasted
1 large ripe avocado, sliced

# White bean, grilled pepper and mozzarella burgers with fresh tomato relish

White cannellini beans made into a burger packed with Italian flavours, with an oozing cube of mozzarella in the middle and another on top.

**Makes 4**

Preheat a griddle pan on the hob until hot, or if you have a barbecue going, use that to grill the peppers. Lightly brush a little oil over the pepper wedges, then lay them on the grill and cook until soft and lightly charred all over, about 15 minutes. Roughly chop and set aside. The cooked peppers will keep in the fridge for a few days if you want to get ahead.

When you are ready to make the burgers, pour the rest of the olive oil into a frying pan and add the onion and rosemary and season generously with salt and pepper. Cook over a medium heat for a good 20 minutes, until the onion is soft and lightly caramelised. Stir in the garlic and cook for another minute, then add the beans and peppers and use a potato masher to break them up to a coarse purée. Stir in the Parmesan and scoop the mixture into a shallow bowl. Set aside to cool, then chill in the fridge for an hour to firm up.

While the bean mix is chilling, make the relish by combining all the ingredients in a small bowl.

Shape the chilled bean mixture into 4 even-sized balls, then divide each ball into 2 smaller ones. Flatten one ball to a disc of about 1cm (½ inch) thick, then put a slice of mozzarella in the middle. Press another ball into a disc about 1cm (½ inch) thick and place on top of the cheese, flattening and pressing the edges together so the cheese is completely encased in bean mix. You are aiming for a burger of around 1.5cm (¾ inch) thickness. Repeat with the remaining portions of beans and cheese.

2 large (bell) peppers, red, yellow or orange, deseeded and cut into 4 wedges
3 tbsp olive oil
1 large red onion
2–3 sprigs of rosemary, needles chopped
2 cloves of garlic, crushed
2 x 400g (14oz) cans of cannellini beans, drained and rinsed
25g Parmesan, freshly grated
1 x 125g (4½oz) ball of mozzarella, cut into 8 even-sized slices
2 tbsp plain (all-purpose) flour
2 eggs, lightly beaten
125g (2 cups) fresh breadcrumbs
salt and freshly ground black pepper
vegetable oil, for frying

Put the flour, beaten eggs and breadcrumbs into three separate bowls, ready to coat the burgers.

Dip one burger into the flour, coating all over, then dip into the egg, followed by the breadcrumbs. Set on a plate and repeat with the others.

Pour a thin layer of vegetable oil into a frying pan and set over a high heat on the hob or barbecue. Once hot, add the burgers and fry for a few minutes on each side, until crisp and golden. Once you've turned them over, top with the remaining 4 pieces of cheese so they begin to soften as the burgers finish cooking. Use a spatula to flick a little oil up the sides of the burgers to crisp them a little as they cook.

To serve, place a little rocket and a burger on the base of each bun. Top with a good dollop of relish, top with the bun lid and eat immediately.

**For the tomato relish**

150g (5oz) cherry tomatoes,
   finely diced
1 clove of garlic, crushed (optional)
a small bunch of basil, chopped
1 tbsp balsamic vinegar
1 tbsp olive oil
salt and freshly ground black
   pepper

**To serve**

a handful of rocket (arugula) leaves
4 burger buns, split and lightly
   toasted

# Tofu, mushroom and sesame burgers with kimchi

**In these vegan Korean-inspired burgers, flaxseed replaces egg as a binding ingredient. It is readily available in supermarkets – find it near the nuts and seeds.**

**Makes 4 burgers**

Unwrap the tofu and drain off any liquid. Wrap the block in a triple layer of kitchen paper and rest it on a plate. Put another plate on top, then balance a couple of heavy tins on it to weigh it down. Leave to gently squeeze for a good hour or so, or a few hours in the fridge if you have time. Pressing the tofu firms it up and creates a more structurally sound burger.

Place the mushrooms, onion, garlic and ginger in a food processor and pulse until finely chopped. Pour the sesame oil into a frying pan and set over a medium heat. Once hot, add the mushroom mix, soy sauce and chilli flakes and stir-fry for about 12–15 minutes, until soft and quite dry. The more moisture you can get rid of the firmer your burgers will be. Once cooked, scoop into a bowl and set aside until cool enough to handle.

Stir in the cooked rice and ground flaxseed and season generously with salt and pepper. Unwrap the tofu and use your hands to crumble it into the mixture, then stir it in well. Divide the mix into 4 even-sized balls and put them on a plate.

Put the sesame seeds into a shallow dish. Take one of the balls of burger mix and flatten it in your palm to around 2cm (¾ inch) thick. Gently dip it into the sesame seeds to coat all over. Repeat with the other balls, then chill in the fridge for a couple of hours.

When you are ready to cook, pour a little vegetable oil into a large frying pan and set over a medium-high heat on the hob or barbecue. Once the oil is hot, add the burgers and fry for about 5 minutes each side, until the sesame seeds are crisp and golden.

To serve, place a little lettuce and cucumber on the base of each bun, top with the burgers, add some kimchi and finish with a drizzle of chilli sauce, if you like.

396g (14oz) block of firm tofu (beancurd)
400g (14oz) mushrooms, roughly torn or chopped
1 onion, roughly chopped
2 cloves of garlic, roughly chopped
2.5cm (1 inch) piece of fresh root ginger, roughly chopped
1 tbsp sesame oil
1 tbsp soy sauce
½ tsp chilli flakes (optional)
100g (½ cup) cooked brown rice
25g (¼ cup) ground flaxseed (linseed)
60g (½ cup) sesame seeds, to coat
salt and freshly ground black pepper
3 tbsp vegetable oil, for frying

**To serve**
a handful of crisp lettuce leaves
½ cucumber, sliced
4 brioche burger buns, sliced and lightly toasted
150–200g (¾–1 cup) kimchi, or to taste
sriracha sauce, to taste

# Herby falafel burgers with hummus

Feel free to use shop-bought hummus if you like, but once you've got the food processor out for the falafels it takes barely any time to whizz up the hummus too. Just like the bean burger recipes on pages 40–45, these freeze well.

**Makes 4**

Tip the toasted cumin and coriander seeds into a pestle and mortar or a spice mill and roughly grind.

Put the ground spices into a food processor along with the chilli flakes, chickpeas, spring onions, garlic, parsley, coriander and gram flour. Season generously with salt and pepper and blitz together to blend to a stiff paste.

Scoop on to a plate and divide into 4 equal balls, then flatten each to a burger of around 1.5cm (¾ inch) thick, pressing any cracks together firmly. Put them back on the plate, cover, then chill in the fridge for an hour, or up to 24 hours.

For the hummus, give the food processor bowl a quick rinse, then reassemble and add the chickpeas, garlic, tahini and lemon juice. Blitz until a coarse purée, then, with the motor running, add enough cold water to blend to a smooth creamy paste. Add the olive oil and a good grind of salt and pepper and whizz to combine, then scoop into a bowl.

When you are ready to cook, pour the vegetable oil into the base of a large frying pan and set over a medium-high heat on the hob or barbecue. Once the oil is shimmering hot, add the burgers and fry for about 3 minutes on each side, until golden and crisp.

To serve, spread some hummus inside each pitta and add the burgers. Top with a little tomato and cucumber, sprinkle with chopped coriander and add a sprinkle of chilli flakes, if you like.

1 tbsp cumin seeds, toasted
1 tbsp coriander seeds, toasted
1 tsp chilli flakes
2 x 400g (14oz) cans of chickpeas, rinsed and well drained
1 bunch of spring onions (scallions), roughly chopped
2 cloves of garlic, roughly chopped
a small bunch each of flat-leaf parsley and coriander (cilantro), roughly chopped
4 tbsp gram flour (chickpea flour)
salt and freshly ground black pepper
3 tbsp vegetable oil, for frying

**For the hummus**
400g (14oz) can of chickpeas, drained and rinsed
1 clove of garlic, roughly chopped
3 tbsp tahini
juice of ½ lemon
4–5 tbsp cold water
1 tbsp extra virgin olive oil

**To serve**
4 pitta breads, lightly toasted and split open (ideally round ones, if you can find them)
8 cherry tomatoes, quartered
a few slices of cucumber
a little chopped coriander
chilli flakes (optional)

# VEGETABLE 'STACK' BURGERS

Not proper burgers these, but colourful discs of different veg, grilled to perfection, then layered up with all sorts of tasty extras. All three vegetable stack ideas below can be shoved into buns, traditional burger-style, or eaten 'naked', perhaps with a nice green salad. The butternut recipe in particular doesn't really need a burger bun, as squash is a rather dense and filling vegetable, so instead I usually serve it with toasted pitta breads alongside.

## Courgette and halloumi sliders with tomato and tahini

I make these with slices cut from a fat courgette, cutting the halloumi into similar-sized pieces so that they layer up neatly for sandwiching into mini slider rolls.

**Makes 6 little sliders**

Fire up your barbecue ready for direct grilling, or preheat a cast-iron griddle pan on the hob over a high heat.

Brush the courgette slices all over with the olive oil and crushed garlic, seasoning with a little salt and pepper. Lay them on the grill bars or on the griddle and cook on the first side until lightly charred and starting to become tender, about 8–10 minutes depending on the heat you have. Turn over the slices and top 12 of them with the halloumi, allowing the underside to cook and the halloumi to become soft and warm.

While the courgette is cooking, make the sauce. In a small bowl mix together the sun-dried tomatoes, tahini, lemon zest and herbs. Season with salt and pepper. Spoon this mixture on to the slices of courgette that have no halloumi on them, allowing them to warm up for a couple of minutes or so.

Assemble each stack by layering up the slices in buns, finishing with a final halloumi piece. Squeeze over some lemon juice and add a drizzle of chilli sauce, if you like.

1 fat courgette (zucchini), cut into 18 slices about 5mm (¼ inch) thick
1 tbsp olive oil
1 clove of garlic, crushed
250g (9oz) pack of halloumi, cut into 12 pieces
4 sun-dried tomatoes, finely chopped
4 heaped tsp tahini
zest of 1 lemon, juice reserved
1 tbsp marjoram or oregano leaves, chopped
salt and freshly ground black pepper

**To serve**
6 mini slider rolls, sliced
chilli sauce (optional)

# Honey-grilled aubergine, Gorgonzola and spiced walnuts

Aubergine is a classic grilling vegetable – its spongy flesh soaks up smoky flavours with ease and when brushed with a smidgen of honey they become utterly delicious. The gremolata and nuts add both freshness and crunch to the rich, unctuous aubergine. If blue cheese is not your thing, this works really well with goat's cheese.

**Makes 4**

Fire up your barbecue ready for direct grilling, or set a cast-iron griddle on the hob to heat up.

While the grill or griddle is heating, make the parsley gremolata by mixing everything in a small bowl. Set aside.

Lightly brush the aubergine slices with olive oil and season with salt and pepper. Lay on the hot grill bars or on the griddle and cook until the underside is nicely coloured and the slices are starting to soften. Flip them over and cook on the other side until the slices are tender, about 15–20 minutes.

Once the aubergine is grilling, caramelise the nuts. Set a small heatproof pan on the grill bars or on the hob. Once it's hot, add the walnuts, honey and chilli flakes to taste, along with a little salt. Allow to cook, stirring all the time, until the honey has coated the nuts and they are caramelised and sticky. Keep an eagle eye on them, as they will burn in an instant. Tip the nuts on to a chopping board and roughly chop.

Once the aubergine slices are tender, brush them with a little honey and cook on each side for another minute or so, until they lightly caramelise. Slide the slices away from the heat, top half with the cheese, then shut the lid of the barbecue and leave for a couple of minutes so the cheese begins to melt. If you are cooking on a griddle, transfer the aubergine slices to a plate, top half with the cheese and loosely cover to let it melt.

To serve, put a little rocket on to 4 of the slices of ciabatta, followed by a slice of cheese-covered aubergine and then a plain slice. Sprinkle over a little of the gremolata and some of the nuts. Add the top slices of ciabatta and serve immediately.

2 medium aubergines (eggplants), cut into 1cm (½ inch) thick slices lengthways
2 tbsp olive oil
2 tsp runny honey
150g (5oz) Gorgonzola, cut into cubes
salt and freshly ground black pepper

**For the parsley gremolata**
½ bunch of flat-leaf parsley, finely chopped
zest of 1 lemon
1 clove of garlic, chopped

**For the walnuts**
40g (¼ cup) walnut halves
2 tsp runny honey
½–1 tsp chilli flakes

**To serve**
8 diagonal slices cut from a ciabatta loaf, cut to fit the aubergine slices
a handful of rocket (arugula)

# Sticky butternut squash and feta with pomegranate salsa and garlic yoghurt

Butternut squash grills a treat. I often leave the skin on when I cook squash, born from a combination of loving the chewy texture and being too lazy to peel them. Choose a good, even-shaped squash, so all your slices are of a similar diameter. The slices that have a hole in the middle where the seeds were will make the perfect receptacle for the pomegranate salsa. Almost as if they were designed for that very purpose . . .

**Serves 4**

Fire up your barbecue ready for direct and indirect cooking, or set a griddle pan over a medium heat to get hot.

Brush the squash slices with a little olive oil and season with salt and pepper. Arrange them on the barbecue so they are slightly off to the side of the fire. If you are cooking on a griddle, lower the heat a little. Cook for about 30 minutes, turning them over halfway, or until tender when pierced with the tip of a knife. Brush the pomegranate molasses all over both sides and cook for a few minutes on one side until sticky and caramelised. Turn the squash over and top 4 slices with the crumbled feta, avoiding the slices with the hole so it doesn't fall through! Sprinkle on the Aleppo pepper or chilli flakes and leave to cook for another couple of minutes, until the cheese begins to melt. Shut the barbecue lid or loosely cover the griddle with foil to help.

While the squash is cooking, make the pomegranate salsa by mixing together the pomegranate seeds, spring onions, pomegranate molasses, parsley and mint. Season with salt and pepper and set aside. Make the yoghurt sauce by mixing the yoghurt, garlic and chilli with a little salt and pepper.

To serve, layer up 2 pieces of squash, starting with a feta-topped piece. Spoon over a little of the pomegranate salsa and the yoghurt sauce and serve with the pitta strips alongside.

1 x 1.2–1.4kg (2¾–3lb) butternut squash, cut into 8 approx. 2.5cm (1 inch) rings, skin on, seeds discarded
2 tbsp olive oil
1 tbsp pomegranate molasses
200g (7oz) feta, crumbled
2 tsp Aleppo pepper flakes, or more to taste (or use regular chilli flakes)
salt and freshly ground black pepper

### For the salsa
1 large pomegranate, seeds picked
3 spring onions (scallions), finely chopped
1 tbsp pomegranate molasses
a small bunch of flat-leaf parsley, chopped
a few sprigs of mint, leaves picked and chopped

### For the garlic yoghurt sauce
5 tbsp Greek yoghurt
1 clove of garlic, crushed
1–2 medium hot red chillies, finely chopped

### To serve
4 pitta breads, toasted and cut into strips

# Minted pea and paneer fritters

**Paneer is a mild Indian cheese that is great for cooking, as it doesn't melt on heating. Here it is combined with peas in a colourful, vibrant fritter that can happily be fried up in just a few minutes.**

**Makes 12, serving about 4 as a snack**

Blanch the peas in boiling water for 3–4 minutes, until tender, then drain well. Tip two-thirds of them into a food processor and pulse until coarsely crushed. Alternatively, tip them on to a board and finely chop with a large knife. Scoop into a mixing bowl and add the rest of the peas, along with the paneer, the mint and a generous seasoning of salt and pepper. Crack in the eggs and add the flour, beating well with a wooden spoon until combined.

When you are ready to cook, drizzle a little oil into a large frying pan or plancha and set on the barbecue over the fire, or over a medium-high heat on the hob. Once hot, add a few tablespoons of batter, spacing them out well as they will puff up a little. Cook for around 3 minutes on each side, until golden and crisp. Transfer to a plate lined with kitchen paper and keep hot while you cook the rest.

Serve hot, with a dollop of mango chutney and sprinkled with a little chilli and coriander.

350g (3 cups) frozen peas
225g (8oz) paneer, crumbled
a small bunch of mint, leaves
   thinly sliced
3 large eggs
100g (¾ cup) self-raising flour
   (self-rising flour)
salt and freshly ground black
   pepper
2 tbsp vegetable oil, for shallow
   frying

**To serve**
mango chutney
long green chillies, thinly sliced
a little coriander (cilantro),
   chopped

# Smoky sweetcorn polenta cakes with green tomato salsa

These light-textured corn cakes are so easy and make a great brunch or lunch. If you can't find green tomatoes, seek out the more traditional Mexican tomatillos – you can find them in specialist greengrocers.

**Makes about 12, serving 4 as a snack**

Preheat your barbecue ready for direct grilling, or set a griddle pan on the hob to heat up.

Lightly brush the corn with oil and season all over with salt and pepper. Lay on the hot grill bars or on the griddle and cook for 25–30 minutes, turning regularly until lightly charred all over. Remove to a board and set aside until cool enough to handle.

Meanwhile, brush the green tomatoes with a little of the oil and cook them cut side down on the grill or griddle for about 5 minutes, until lightly charred. Don't try to turn them too early or they may stick to the grill. Flip them over and cook for another 5 minutes. Remove to a chopping board, finely chop and place in a bowl. Stir in the rest of the olive oil and the spring onions, garlic, coriander, chillies, lime juice and caster sugar. Season with salt and pepper and set aside.

Use a sharp knife to slice off the cooled corn kernels and tip them into a mixing bowl. Add the yoghurt, polenta, spring onions, coriander and eggs. Season really well with salt and pepper and stir together thoroughly. Set aside.

Set a frying pan or plancha on your barbecue or hob and leave it to get really hot for a good 10 minutes. Once hot, drizzle on a little oil and use a scrunched-up piece of kitchen paper to spread it into a very thin layer.

When you are ready to cook, quickly beat the bicarbonate of soda through the batter. Spoon mounds of the batter on to the plancha or pan, leaving space between them. Cook for a couple of minutes on each side. Transfer to a plate and loosely cover to keep warm while you cook the rest. To serve, top each corn cake with a little salsa and eat while warm.

2 corn on the cob, grilled until golden (yields 250g/1½ cups corn)
1 tsp olive oil, plus a little extra for frying
200g (1½ cups) Greek yoghurt
100g (⅔ cup) instant polenta (cornmeal)
½ bunch of spring onions (scallions), thinly sliced
⅔ big bunch of coriander (cilantro), chopped
2 large eggs
1 tsp bicarbonate of soda (baking soda)
salt and freshly ground black pepper

**For the green tomato salsa**
250g (9oz) green tomatoes, cut in half
2 tbsp olive oil
½ bunch of spring onions, finely chopped
1–2 cloves of garlic, crushed, to taste
⅓ big bunch of coriander, chopped
1–2 green chillies, finely chopped, to taste
juice of 1 lime
½–1 tsp caster sugar, to taste

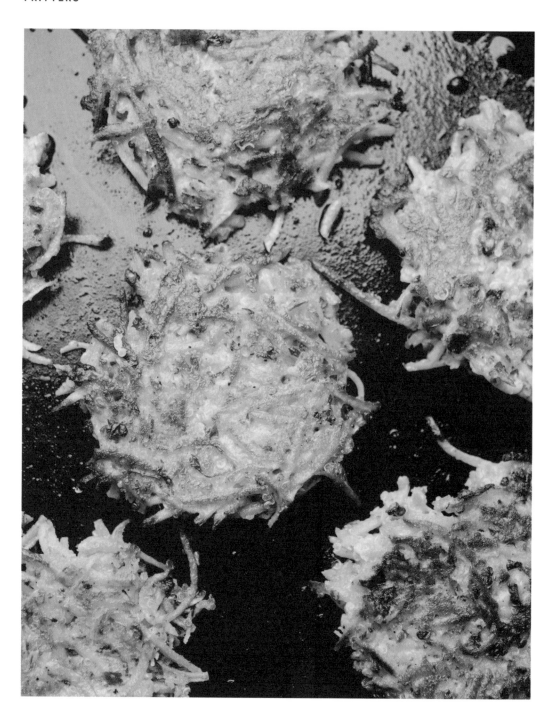

# Sweet potato and quinoa rösti with coconut cream dressing

Sweet potato has a lot less starch than regular potato, so
these fritters are delicate little blighters. The flour helps to
bind them together, but you will still get little straggly bits
around the edges. Just don't scrimp on the oil when frying
– crispy edges are surely the main point of a rösti!

**Makes about 12–14, serving about 4 as a snack**

Tip the quinoa into a small pan and crumble in the stock cube.
Pour over enough boiling water to cover the quinoa by 1cm
(½ inch). Set over a high heat and simmer until just tender,
about 12–15 minutes. Drain well and tip into a mixing bowl.

Add the sweet potato, most of the coriander (reserving a little to
garnish), the gram flour and water, and season generously with
salt and pepper. Stir well to mix and set aside for 15 minutes for
the flour to absorb the water.

Meanwhile, make the dressing by pouring the coconut cream
into a mixing bowl and whisking until smooth. Add the ginger,
turmeric and lime juice and whisk once more, seasoning with a
little salt to taste. Set aside.

When you are ready to cook, set a large frying pan on the
barbecue, or over a medium-high heat on the hob. Once the oil
is hot, add spoonfuls of the rösti mix to the pan, pressing them
down so they are around 1cm (½ inch) thick. Cook for about
2–3 minutes on each side, until crisp, then transfer to a plate
lined with kitchen paper to keep warm while you cook the rest.
Add extra oil to the pan if necessary.

Sprinkle with the chilli and coriander and serve with the
dressing alongside.

100g (½ cup) quinoa
½ vegetable stock cube
500–600g (18–21oz) sweet
    potatoes, peeled and grated
    (about 1 large)
a generous handful of coriander
    (cilantro), chopped
100g (¾ cup) gram flour
    (chickpea flour)
75ml (⅓ cup) water
salt and freshly ground black
    pepper
4 tbsp vegetable oil, for shallow
    frying

**For the coconut dressing**
250ml (8fl oz) carton of coconut
    cream
30g (1oz) fresh root ginger, finely
    grated
15g (½oz) fresh turmeric root,
    finely grated, or 1 tsp ground
    turmeric
juice of ½–1 lime, to taste
salt, to taste

**To garnish**
1–2 bird's-eye chillies, thinly
    sliced
a little coriander, chopped

# Carrot and cumin fritters with tahini and coriander yoghurt

**So quick and easy to make, these spiced carrot fritters are made with protein-rich gram (chickpea) flour, which is now readily available in bigger supermarkets.**

**Makes about 12–14, serving 4**

Stir together the carrot and onion in a mixing bowl, then add the gram flour, water, eggs, cumin and smoked paprika. Season well with salt and pepper and beat together until evenly combined. Set aside for 20 minutes.

For the sauce, stir together the yoghurt, tahini, garlic and coriander and season to taste with salt and pepper.

When you are ready to cook, set a plancha, or a heavy-based frying pan, over the barbecue or on the hob. Heat for about 7–10 minutes, or until a few drops of water sizzle instantly.

Once hot, brush the plancha or pan with a little vegetable oil. Use a tablespoon to drop in dollops of carrot batter and cook for about 2–3 minutes each side. Reduce the heat a little if they are browning too quickly. Transfer to a plate and keep warm while you cook the rest of the fritters.

Serve hot, with a little of the yoghurt sauce spooned over and a sprinkling of red chilli.

250g (9oz) carrots, coarsely grated
1 medium red onion, finely chopped
100g (1 cup) gram flour (chickpea flour)
100ml (⅓ cup) cold water
2 large eggs
1 tbsp cumin seeds, toasted and roughly ground
1 tsp smoked paprika
salt and freshly ground black pepper
a little vegetable oil, for frying
a little chopped red chilli, to garnish

**For the tahini and coriander yogurt**
200g (1½ cups) Greek yoghurt
3 tbsp tahini
1 clove of garlic, crushed
a generous handful of coriander (cilantro), chopped

# Panelle, grilled Romano peppers, avocado and egg

**Panelle are crisp chickpea flour fritters from Sicily. Stacked with grilled peppers and avocado and topped with a fried egg, they make a perfect brunch dish. Make the batter the day before and chill it overnight so it's an easy cook-and-assemble job the following morning.**

### Serves 4

Set a heavy-based pan over a medium heat and add the oil, garlic, fennel and chilli flakes. Fry for a minute or so, then pour in the water and turn up the heat so it comes to a steady boil. Once boiling, reduce the heat to a minimum and slowly pour in the sifted gram flour, whisking constantly so it forms a smooth paste. Stir constantly for a few minutes until the batter thickens and starts to come away from the edges of the pan. Remove from the heat and season well with salt and pepper.

Take two 30cm (12 inch) square baking trays and line each with a sheet of clingfilm. Divide the batter between the trays and spread it out as best you can. Top each with another sheet of clingfilm and press on to the surface, smoothing and flattening it with your hands so it forms a thin, even layer around 5mm (¼ inch) thick. Set aside to cool, then transfer to the fridge to chill completely.

When you are ready to cook, fire up the barbecue ready for direct grilling or set a griddle pan on the hob to heat up. Brush the Romano peppers lightly with a little oil and set on the grill or griddle. Cook for around 10–15 minutes, turning them over a couple of times, until they are soft and charred in places.

While the peppers are grilling, halve the avocados and scoop out the flesh. Dice into 1–2cm (½–¾ inch) pieces, putting them into a bowl as you go. Add most of the basil (reserving a little to garnish), drizzle in the balsamic vinegar and season with salt and pepper. Stir to mix, roughly crushing the avocado as you go.

Set a heavy-based frying pan on the hob or barbecue. Add about 3–5mm (⅛–¼ inch) of oil and leave to heat up until shimmering hot.

### For the panelle
2 tbsp olive oil, plus extra for frying
2 cloves of garlic, crushed
2 tsp fennel seeds, crushed in a pestle and mortar
a pinch of chilli flakes
750ml (3¼ cups) water
250g (2 cups) gram flour (chickpea flour), sifted
salt and freshly ground black pepper

### To serve
3 large Romano peppers, sliced in half lengthways and deseeded, then cut in half crossways
1 tsp olive oil
3 large ripe avocados
a small pack of basil, leaves roughly chopped
2 tbsp balsamic vinegar
4 eggs
olive oil, for shallow frying

Take the trays of panelle and slice each into 8 pieces. Once the
oil is hot, fry the pieces in batches for about 2–3 minutes each
side, until crisp and golden; transfer them to a plate lined with
kitchen paper as you go. Cover with a few more sheets of kitchen
paper to keep the panelle warm while you cook the others.

Once all the panelle are cooked, crack 4 eggs into the frying pan
and fry until they are cooked to your liking.

To serve, build a stack on each of 4 warmed plates, alternating
layers of panelle with avocado and pepper and finishing with a
fried egg. Scatter over a little of the reserved basil and add a final
drizzle of balsamic. Eat immediately.

# CHEESE TOASTIES

Grilled vegetables are the perfect thing for layering up with your favourite cheese, in (guess what!) a grilled sandwich. I almost always make cheese toasties for just one – it's the sort of indulgent yet speedy treat that is often best satisfied on your own. Good sourdough bread is perhaps a little impractical here, as all those holes play havoc with the ooze, but surely the melty, crispy stuck-on bits of cheese are the main point. I urge you to brace yourself for a bit of mess and washing-up after, it will be well worth it.

## Charred asparagus and Cambozola toastie

I adore blue cheese in any shape or form, and German Brie-style Cambozola is no exception. If you're not such a fan, feel free to substitute regular Brie or Camembert.

### Serves 1

Fire up your barbecue ready for direct grilling, or preheat a griddle pan on the hob.

Drizzle a tiny bit of olive oil over the asparagus and rub all over to coat. Season with a little salt and pepper. Spread the asparagus out on your griddle or barbecue and cook until lightly charred and just tender, about 6–7 minutes depending on the thickness. Remove from the grill and set aside.

Lightly butter your bread, you don't need much. Turn one slice over and arrange the grilled asparagus on top. Lay the cheese on top of that and top with the other slice of bread, again with the buttered side facing outwards. Using a combination of tongs and a fish slice, carefully transfer the sandwich to the grill and toast for a couple of minutes on each side, or until the bread is crisp and the cheese is starting to explode a bit out of the edges. Remove to a board, slice in half and allow to cool for just a minute or so before tucking in.

a drizzle of olive oil
6 spears of asparagus, washed and trimmed
a slick of butter
2 generous slices of sourdough bread
100g (3½oz) Cambozola, cut into 2 thick slices
salt and freshly ground black pepper

# Rainbow chard, Cheddar and mango chutney

Chard is a very lovely thing to grill, the earthy flavours responding brilliantly to heat and smoke. You need to treat the stems and leaves almost as two separate vegetables, as the stems take considerably longer to cook. I tend to put them on to a cold griddle, then turn on the heat so they start with a few minutes of gentle cooking as the temperature rises. Of course, if you are cooking over charcoal this isn't practical, so start them off on a colder part of your barbecue before moving them over the direct heat once they have started to soften.

**Serves 1**

Drizzle a little oil over the stems and leaves of the chard, rubbing it in so they are evenly coated. Rest the stems on your griddle and turn on the heat so they begin to soften as it comes up to temperature, or set them on the grill, slightly away from the fire. Turn them over regularly as they cook so they caramelise all over. Once the stems are almost cooked, about 10 minutes, add the leaves to the hot grill and allow them to wilt and start to char in places.

Spread just a little butter on both slices of bread. Turn one slice over and layer on the grilled chard leaves. Roughly chop the stems and toss together on the chopping board with the chilli. Scatter them over the leaves and top with the Cheddar. Turn over the other slice of bread and spread the mango chutney on the unbuttered side, then invert over the sandwich and press down firmly so the buttered side is on top. Transfer to the grill carefully, using a fish slice and tongs to keep everything together, and cook for a couple of minutes each side. It's ready when the bread is nicely toasted and the cheese is melting. Slice in half and allow to cool for a minute or so before eating – the molten cheese will be burn-your-tongue hot.

a drizzle of olive oil

4 stalks of rainbow chard, stems and leaves separated

a slick of butter

2 generous slices of sourdough bread

1 bird's-eye chilli, finely chopped, or more to taste

75g (2½oz) extra mature Cheddar

1 tbsp mango chutney

salt and freshly ground black pepper

# Low, slow and smoked

# Smoked Parmesan parsnips, fennel butter, hazelnuts

The star of this dish is the complex and earthy fennel butter. If you have some glowing coals left after cooking, it's fun to use tongs to place one on top of the butter slices to melt and sizzle as you bring to the dish to the table.

### Serves 4

Fire up the barbecue ready for indirect grilling. Once it's up to temperature, throw on some smoking wood chunks or chips and allow them to catch and smoulder.

Tip the parsnips into a fireproof roasting tin, drizzle with the olive oil, season with a little salt and pepper and toss to mix. Rest the tin on the barbecue, well away from the fire. Shut the lid to allow maximum bathing in the smoke. Cook for 45–50 minutes, rotating the tin once or twice and tossing the parsnips about to ensure they are cooking evenly. Add more wood chunks or chips as necessary to keep a fairly constant smoke going.

Meanwhile, make the fennel butter. Tip the fennel seeds into a small frying pan and set over a medium-high heat on the hob to toast for a couple of minutes. Transfer to a pestle and mortar and crush to a coarse powder. Add the softened butter and honey and mix together, along with a little salt and pepper. Scoop into a bowl and set aside.

Once the parsnips are tender and lightly coloured, remove the tin from the barbecue, shutting the lid to keep the heat in. Sprinkle over the Parmesan and toss to coat evenly. Remove the parsnips one by one and rest them directly on the grill bars over the fire. Cook for about 7–10 minutes, turning regularly, until they are deeply golden and crisp.

Put the parsnips on a serving plate. Scatter with the hazelnuts and thyme leaves. Top the parsnips with dollops of fennel butter, adding a few glowing coals to melt the butter if you like (see above). Serve immediately.

1kg (2lb 3oz) fat parsnips, peeled
    and cut into quarters lengthways
1 tbsp olive oil
50g (2oz) Parmesan, freshly grated
50g (½ cup) hazelnuts, toasted and
    roughly chopped
a few sprigs of thyme, leaves picked
salt and freshly ground black
    pepper

### For the fennel butter
1 heaped tbsp fennel seeds
75g (3oz) butter, slightly softened
1 tbsp runny honey

# Smoked whole celeriac

**Smoked celeriac is a revelation – the long, slow cooking process creates a meltingly tender centre while the skin becomes deliciously crisp and not unlike a roast potato. This makes an impressive side dish to any roast.**

**Serves 4–6 as a side dish**

Preheat your barbecue ready for indirect grilling. Once it is up to temperature, add a few smoking wood chunks to the fire.

Give the celeriac a good scrub under running water, paying particular attention to the root area. Cut a thin slice off the top and bottom and use a sharp knife to carefully slash a few cuts really deep into the flesh on both sides to allow the oil to penetrate into the vegetable as it cooks. Carefully spike the metal skewers through the centre of the celeriac, piercing it all the way through and out the other side. The metal skewers will help transfer the barbecue's heat deep into the celeriac and speed up the cooking process.

Take a double square of foil and set the skewered celeriac in the centre. Scrunch up the sides to form a shallow 'dish' that will catch the coriander oil as you baste it over the celeriac. Rest the celeriac on the opposite side of the barbecue to the fire.

Tip the crushed coriander seeds and olive oil into a small barbecue-proof pan, along with a good grind of salt and pepper. Rest the pan next to the celeriac, away from the fire, and brush a little oil over the top, then shut the barbecue lid.

Every 30 minutes or so, lift the lid, baste a bit more oil all over the celeriac and add a little more charcoal and smoking wood to keep the fire gently smouldering. Leave the celeriac to cook for a good 3½–4 hours, until really tender throughout.

Place the celeriac in the centre of a serving dish and pour over any coriander oil from the bottom of the cooking foil. Slice into wedges to serve.

1 whole celeriac, about 750–800g (26–28oz) (trimmed weight)
1 tbsp coriander seeds, toasted and roughly ground
100ml (⅓ cup) extra virgin olive oil
salt and freshly ground black pepper

**You also need**
3 metal skewers

# Baked sweet potatoes, Sri Lankan-spiced caramelised red onions

**Cutting sweet potatoes in half before cooking means they soak up some smoke from the barbecue as they gently bake. Here they get topped generously with sweet spiced onions for a hearty lunch.**

### Serves 2

Fire up the barbecue ready for indirect grilling. Once the coals are ready to cook, throw on some smoking wood chunks or chips. The potatoes get cooked for a long time, so be prepared to add extra charcoal and smoking wood as necessary.

Slice the sweet potatoes in half lengthways and make a few diagonal slashes through the cut sides, penetrating about halfway through each potato. Brush the cut side with the sesame oil and season with a little salt and pepper. Lay them cut side down on the grill bars, away from the fire, then shut the lid and leave to smoke and soften for about an hour. Turn the potatoes over and cook skin side down until tender all the way through – about another 45 minutes, depending on how hot your fire is.

Once you have turned the sweet potato halves, set a heatproof frying pan directly over the fire and add the sesame oil, mustard seeds and chilli flakes, frying them for a minute or so. Add the onions, butter and the crushed cumin, cardamom seeds and cloves, stirring as the butter melts. Season with a little salt and pepper, then shut the lid of the barbecue and cook for about 40 minutes. Stir a couple of times to make sure they are cooking evenly – they are ready when they are really soft, lightly caramelised and fragrant.

To serve, put 2 potato halves on each plate and top with some onions. Add a generous dollop of yoghurt and scatter over a little coriander and chilli.

2 sweet potatoes, about 350–400g (12–14oz) each
2 tsp sesame oil
salt and freshly ground black pepper

### For the spiced onions

2 tbsp sesame oil
1 tbsp mustard seeds
1 tsp chilli flakes
500g (1lb 2oz) red onions, thinly sliced
50g (2oz) butter
1 heaped tsp cumin seeds, roughly crushed in a pestle and mortar
2 cardamom pods, seeds scraped out and roughly crushed in a pestle and mortar
4 cloves, roughly crushed in a pestle and mortar

### To serve

4 tbsp thick full-fat yoghurt
a little coriander (cilantro), chopped
1–2 hot red chillies, finely chopped, to taste

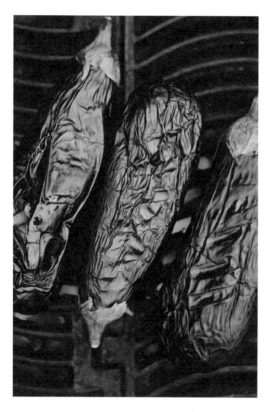

# Best ever baba ganoush with flatbread chips

**Baba ganoush is one of my favourite ever dips, and by cooking the aubergines over a wood fire you get an even more intensely smoky flavour. Baba ganoush on steroids.**

**Serves about 4 as a dip**

Fire up the barbecue for direct and indirect grilling and, once hot, add a few chunks of wood to the fire to get some good smoke going.

Prick the aubergines all over with a fork and lay them on the grill bars, directly over the fire. Cook for around an hour, turning and rotating them a few times until the outsides are darkly charred and the aubergines are collapsed and very soft. If they are burning too much before softening, slide them slightly away from the fire. Once they are cooked, remove them and leave to cool down so you can handle them.

Slice the aubergines in half and scoop out the flesh, spooning it into a food processor as you go. Add the garlic, tahini, lemon juice, olive oil and salt and pepper and blitz until velvety smooth. You can also put it all into a deep jug and purée with a stick blender. Transfer to a serving bowl and set aside.

To make the flatbread chips, preheat the oven to 180°C fan/400°F. You can also cook them on the barbecue if there is still plenty of heat to be had. Lay the flatbreads in a stack on a chopping board and use a sharp knife to slice them through into 8 triangular-shaped wedges, just like cutting a cake. Spread them out over a couple of baking sheets and drizzle with the oil. Sprinkle over the crushed cumin and chilli and season with a little salt and pepper. Slide the trays into the oven and bake until crisp, about 5–7 minutes. Alternatively, lay the wedges directly on to the grill bars and shut the lid. Depending on the heat of the fire they may take less time to crisp, or even a little longer if it's a touch cool.

To serve, scatter the Aleppo pepper and parsley over the baba ganoush and add a good drizzle of olive oil. Serve with the chips.

3 large aubergines (eggplants), about 350g (12oz) each
3 cloves of garlic, roughly chopped
1 heaped tbsp tahini
juice of 1 lemon
4 tbsp extra virgin olive oil, plus a little extra for drizzling
1 tsp Aleppo pepper or regular chilli flakes
a few sprigs of flat-leaf parsley, chopped

### For the flatbread chips
6 flatbreads
2 tbsp olive oil
1 tbsp cumin seeds, crushed
1–2 tsp chilli flakes
salt and freshly ground black pepper

# Smoked mushrooms with sherry and garlic cream

Mushrooms' dense flesh and the large surface area of the gills make them very effective sponges for absorbing delicious smoky flavours from the fire. Combine them with an easy but rich sauce and you have a most luxurious dish. I used Portobellini mushrooms here, but feel free to use any mix of 'shrooms that takes your fancy.

**Serves 2**

Make a simple marinade for the mushrooms by mixing the olive oil, sherry vinegar, parsley and a grind of salt and pepper in a large bowl. Add the mushrooms and toss together gently until evenly coated. Set aside for an hour or so.

When you are ready to cook, fire up your barbecue for indirect grilling. When it is up to temperature, add a little smoking wood to the charcoal and allow it to catch fire.

Pop the whole garlic cloves on the grill bars off to one side of the fire, and roast until charred on the outside and soft and squidgy when you give them a little squeeze, about 15–20 minutes.

At the same time, put the mushrooms face down on the grill, away from the fire. Reserve the leftover marinade. Shut the lid and leave to smoke for 15 minutes, then turn the mushrooms over and cook on the other side for another 20 minutes. They are ready when they are soft to the touch and shrunken in size by around a third.

Remove the garlic and leave to cool a little, then squeeze the flesh from the skins into a small heatproof pan. Add the reserved marinade, and stir in the cream and sherry. Set the pan on the barbecue, directly over the fire, and shut the lid. Allow to bubble for a good 10 minutes, stirring once or twice. Move the pan to a cool part of the barbecue to keep warm.

Lightly brush the bread with a little oil – you won't need much – and set over the fire to toast for a couple of minutes each side.

To serve, pile the smoked mushrooms on the toast and pour over the sauce. Add a good grind of black pepper, sprinkle over a little chopped parsley, and tuck in straight away.

2 tbsp olive oil
1 tbsp sherry vinegar
a handful of flat-leaf parsley, chopped
300g (10½oz) mushrooms
2 fat cloves of garlic, whole and unpeeled
150ml (⅔ cup) double (heavy) cream
50ml Oloroso sherry
salt and freshly ground black pepper

**To serve**
3–4 slices of sourdough bread
a drizzle of olive oil
a little chopped flat-leaf parsley, to garnish

# Smoked onion soup, black olives, thyme

**The humble onion is one of my favourite vegetables and it's rare a day goes by without me reaching for one in my cooking. Here they get the long, slow smoky treatment on the barbecue before being whizzed into a rich soup.**

**Serves 4–6**

Fire up your barbecue ready for indirect cooking. Once hot, throw on some smoking wood chunks.

Meanwhile, prepare the onions. Leaving the skin on, cut a 1cm (½ inch) slice off the top of each onion, then carefully cut vertically down two-thirds of the way through to the root. Turn the onion through 90 degrees and cut again, then turn and cut twice more to end up with 8 wedges all connected to the root. Arrange cut side up in an old roasting tin so they sit snugly together. Drizzle over the olive oil and season with a little salt and pepper.

Set the tin of onions on the grill bars, away from the fire and shut the lid. Leave to smoke for 1½ hours, rotating the tin every 30 minutes and adding more fuel and smoking wood as necessary. Cover the tin snugly with foil and shut the lid once more, leaving them to cook for another hour, or until soft and tender. Cook them for longer if necessary – once covered with foil you would be hard pushed to overcook them. Remove from the barbecue and allow to cool a little.

Once cool enough to handle, pull away and discard the outer skin and roots. Roughly chop the flesh and scoop into a large pan. Add the butter and most of the thyme leaves and set over a medium-low heat on the hob. Season with salt and pepper and fry gently for about 10 minutes. Stir in the flour thoroughly, then pour in the milk and turn up the heat. Bring to the boil, stirring all the time as the soup thickens. Simmer steadily for about 5 minutes, then stir in the cream. Turn off the heat and use a stick blender to purée until smooth.

To serve, pour into warmed bowls and scatter over the olives and remaining thyme leaves.

1kg (2lb 3oz) medium-sized onions
1 tbsp olive oil
50g (2oz) butter
a few sprigs of thyme, leaves stripped and roughly chopped
25g (1 tbsp) plain flour (all-purpose flour)
500ml (2 cups) milk
150ml (⅔ cup) double (heavy) cream
salt and freshly ground black pepper

**To serve**
a few black olives, chopped
a few sprigs of thyme, leaves picked

# Smoked cauliflower, spiced garlic butter

Cauliflowers are having something of a renaissance at the moment and are happily no longer just the preserve of cauliflower cheese. However, I still think they benefit from the richness of something dairy-related, so here they get doused in rather an unseemly quantity of butter.

**Serves 4–6**

Fire up the barbecue ready for indirect grilling. While the charcoal is getting to temperature, bring a really large pan of lightly salted water to the boil on the hob.

Put the cauliflower leaves and stem pieces into a mixing bowl, and toss with a little olive oil, salt and pepper, then set aside. Cut a thin sliver off the base of the cauliflower so it sits nice and level, then carefully lower it into the boiling water and blanch for 5 minutes. Drain well and place in a sturdy roasting tin. Drizzle a little oil over the cauliflower and season with salt and pepper.

Once the barbecue is ready for cooking, add a few lumps of smoking wood or a handful of smoking chips. Rest the tin away from the fire and shut the lid. Cook for an hour, checking once or twice, and rotating the tin so it cooks evenly. After an hour, loosely cover the cauliflower with foil to prevent it drying out – it should have absorbed lots of lovely smoke flavours – and cook for a further 45–60 minutes, or until tender when pierced with the tip of a knife.

To make the spiced butter, mash together the soft butter, garlic, chopped herbs, cumin seeds and chilli, if using, and add a little salt and pepper to taste.

Remove the foil from the cauliflower and tip in the chopped stems and leaves, spreading them out in the tin. Use a knife to spread the butter over the surface of the cauliflower and move the tin directly over the fire. Cook for a further 15–20 minutes, until the butter has melted and the stems are tender but still with bite.

To serve, lift the cauliflower on to a plate and spoon over the wilted stems and butter.

1 large cauliflower, leaves and stems trimmed off and sliced into bite-sized pieces
1 tbsp olive oil
125g (4oz) butter, softened
2 cloves of garlic, crushed
a handful of fresh oregano or marjoram sprigs, leaves picked and chopped
1 heaped tbsp cumin seeds, bruised in a pestle and mortar
1–2 tsp chipotle chilli flakes (optional)
salt and freshly ground black pepper

# Smoked Jerusalem artichokes, charred rosemary mayonnaise

**These knobbly little tubers turn soft, tender and intensely savoury when given the low and slow treatment. Charred rosemary mayo is spectacularly good and will go with all manner of dishes – it will keep in the fridge for 5 days.**

**Serves 4–6**

Fire up the barbecue ready for indirect cooking. Once it's up to temperature, throw on some smoking wood chunks or chips.

Slice the artichokes into halves or quarters depending on their size, putting them into an old roasting tin as you go. Drizzle in the oil and season with salt and pepper, tossing to mix. Set the tin on the barbecue away from the fire and leave to smoke for an hour, until tender. Check them a couple of times, rotating the tin and tossing them about a bit so they cook evenly.

Lay the rosemary sprigs directly over the fire and shut the lid. Allow them to char for a minute or two, until lightly blackened but not burnt. Remove from the barbecue and shut the lid so the artichokes keep smoking. Pick the charred rosemary needles from the stalks and finely chop. Set aside.

Put the egg yolk, mustard, garlic and a good grind of salt and pepper into a mixing bowl. Use an electric whisk to blend together for a few seconds. Measure both oils into a jug and add a few drops to the egg yolk mixture, whisking constantly. Once it's combined, add a few more drops and whisk again. Keep whisking and adding oil a little at a time until it you have used it all, then whisk in the chopped rosemary and white wine vinegar. Scoop into a serving bowl and chill until needed.

Once the artichokes are tender, use tongs to lift them from the roasting tin directly on to the grill bars above the fire and allow them to crisp up for about 10 minutes, turning a couple of times.

Scatter the leaves and herbs over a serving plate and top with the hot artichokes. Drizzle over a little mayonnaise and serve straight away.

1kg (2lb 3oz) Jerusalem artichokes, well scrubbed under running water
2 tbsp olive oil
3–4 handfuls of mixed leaves
a handful of soft herbs (dill, basil, parsley or chives are all good)
salt and freshly ground black pepper

**For the mayonnaise**

3 sprigs of rosemary, to taste
1 large egg yolk
2 tsp English mustard
1 clove of garlic, crushed
100ml (1/3 cup) neutral oil, e.g. groundnut or vegetable oil
25ml (1/8 cup) extra virgin olive oil
2 tbsp white wine vinegar

# Grilled globe artichokes

The smokiness of the fire adds so much flavour to artichokes that once you've tried them grilled I doubt you'll eat them any other way. Pull off the individual petals one at a time, dipping the base into the flavoured oil and teasing out the flesh with your teeth. Eventually you will get to the heart of the artichoke, then dip the whole thing into the oil and eat with gusto.

**Serves 4**

Prepare the artichokes. Set a large pan of lightly salted water to boil. Remove any leaves from the stems of the artichokes, then use scissors to snip off the sharp ends of the outer leaves. Use a sharp knife to cut off a good centimetre (½ inch) from the top of each artichoke, then slice through the stem to give you two halves. Douse the cut edge immediately in lemon juice to prevent browning – artichokes oxidise very quickly. Use a teaspoon to scoop out and discard the furry 'choke' from each side, again wiping a little lemon juice over the exposed surface. Repeat with the other 3 artichokes.

Once all the artichokes have been prepared, plunge them into the pan of boiling water and blanch them for 15 minutes. Drain well, then brush the surface all over with a little olive oil.

Fire up your barbecue for indirect grilling. Once it's ready, add some smoking wood chips or small chunks of wood.

Rest the artichoke halves on the grill bars cut side down, arranging them slightly away from the fire. Shut the lid and leave to cook for 20 minutes, until nicely charred, moving them around once or twice to keep them cooking evenly.

Mix the oil, parsley and garlic in a small frying pan, seasoning generously with salt and pepper.

Turn over the artichokes and use a silicon brush to baste a little parsley and garlic oil on to the cut face. Keep grilling for another 15–20 minutes or so, until the underside is charred.

To serve, arrange the artichokes on a plate and spoon a little oil into the cavity in each half. Serve the rest of the oil in a dish alongside, to dip into.

4 globe artichokes
juice of 1 lemon
150ml (⅔ cup) extra virgin olive oil, plus a little to brush the artichokes
a generous handful of flat-leaf parsley, finely chopped
3 cloves of garlic, finely chopped
salt and freshly ground black pepper

# Slow-cooked swede wedges, Jack Daniels and peppercorn cream sauce

Swede is a tough, dense vegetable, so don't be surprised that it takes a long time to become tender. This makes a great side dish to a winter roast.

**Serve 4–6 as a side dish**

Fire up the barbecue ready for indirect cooking. Once it's up to temperature, throw on some smoking wood chunks or chips.

Spread out the swede wedges in an old roasting tin so that they are in a slightly overlapping single layer. Drizzle over the oil and season with salt and pepper. Rest the tin on the barbecue, away from the fire, and shut the lid. Leave to cook for around an hour and a half. Check occasionally, rotating the tin and turning the wedges so they smoke evenly. If the swede looks like it's beginning to dry out, cover the tin with foil to finish cooking. Add more charcoal and smoking wood or chips as necessary.

Once the swede is tender, remove the wedges one by one to the grill bars above the fire. Allow them to colour and crisp for about 7–8 minutes, turning them regularly. Then slide them away from the fire so they keep warm while you make the sauce.

Put the butter into a heatproof skillet and set on the grill bars above the fire. Once melted, add the garlic and cook for a couple of minutes, then pour in the Jack Daniels and allow it to bubble and reduce by half. Pour in the cream and add the pepper, nutmeg and a little salt, stirring while the sauce heats through.

Use tongs to remove the swede wedges to a warmed serving plate and drizzle over the sauce. Scatter over a little parsley and serve while hot.

750–800g (26–28oz) swede (rutabaga), cut into 1.5cm (¾ inch) wedges
1 tbsp olive oil
a little flat-leaf parsley, chopped
salt and freshly ground black pepper

### For the sauce
25g (1oz) butter
2 cloves of garlic, crushed
3 tbsp Jack Daniels
200ml (¾ cup) double (heavy) cream
1–2 tsp black peppercorns, coarsely crushed
a good pinch of freshly grated nutmeg

# Smoked beetroot, boiled egg, dill and horseradish

Lighting a barbecue just to smoke a bunch of beetroot might seem rather indulgent, and once they are midway through cooking you may question my sanity. Please trust me: as they smoke, they shrink and shrivel by about a third, which concentrates their earthy flavour intensely.

**Serves 2–4, as lunch or a starter**

Fire up your barbecue, setting it up for indirect cooking. Once it is ready to cook, add a few smoking wood chunks or chips.

Spread out the beetroot on the barbecue, away from the fire, and shut the lid. Leave to cook for a good couple of hours, checking every 30 minutes or so and moving them around so they cook evenly. Once they are tender when you pierce with the tip of a knife, remove them from the barbecue and set aside until cool enough to handle. Peel, using a small paring knife to help if necessary, then chop into bite-sized pieces. Put into a bowl and set aside.

Make the dressing by putting the olive oil, horseradish and lemon juice into a bowl and whisking together. Stir in the dill and season to taste with the sugar, salt and pepper. Set aside.

Put the eggs into a small pan and pour in enough cold water to cover them by a couple of centimetres (an inch or so). Set the pan over the hob and bring to the boil. Once boiling, turn the heat down to a simmer and cook for 4 minutes. Drain and run under cold water to stop the cooking, then peel and slice in half.

To assemble the salad, scatter a few leaves on to a large plate (or divide into portions over several plates) and add the cucumber slices. Top with the egg halves and beetroot. Drizzle over the dressing and garnish with a few bits of the reserved dill. Finish with a final grind of black pepper and serve.

8–10 smallish whole beetroots (beets) (between a golfball and a satsuma in size), trimmed with 2cm (¾ inch) stem left intact, and scrubbed under running water
4 eggs
a couple of handfuls of soft leaves, such as lamb's lettuce or round lettuce
½ cucumber, very thinly sliced

**For the dressing**
4 tbsp extra virgin olive oil
1 tbsp hot horseradish sauce
juice of 1 lemon
1 small bunch of dill, chopped (reserve a sprig for garnishing)
1 tsp caster sugar
salt and freshly ground black pepper

# Smoked carrot and caraway dip with rye crispbread

**The dry heat of the barbecue really intensifies and concentrates carrots' flavour. You do need a little time to make the crispbreads, so feel free to replace them with the baked flatbread chips on page 79.**

**Serves 4–6**

For the crispbread, measure the flours into a mixing bowl. Stir in the nigella seeds, salt and yeast. Pour in the water, stirring until it comes together as a stiff dough with no loose flour. Cover the bowl with a tea towel and leave to prove for an hour.

Meanwhile, fire up the barbecue ready for direct and indirect grilling. Once it is up to heat, set a heavy plancha directly over the fire and shut the lid, leaving to heat for 10 minutes.

Tip the dough on to a well-floured worktop and cut into 10 even-sized pieces. Roll out each piece to about 20cm (8 inches) in diameter. Layer them on sheets of baking paper and take to the barbecue. Lay one or two on the hot plancha and shut the lid. Cook for about 5 minutes, then turn over and shut the lid again. They are done when they are deep brown and crisp all the way through. Cook in batches, transferring them to a plate to cool down. You can also bake them in a hot oven (200°C fan/425°F), where they will take around 10 minutes per batch.

Once all the crispbreads are cooked, add a few smoking wood chunks to the fire and leave to catch for a few minutes.

Tip the carrots into an old roasting tin so they fit snugly in a double layer. Drizzle in the oil, add the caraway seeds and season with salt and pepper, tossing to coat. Set on the barbecue away from the fire. Shut the lid and cook until the carrots are really tender, about 1½ hours . Every 30 minutes, lift the lid and give the tin a shake to mix up the carrots, and add more smoking wood as necessary.

Once the carrots are tender, tip them into a food processor and add the cream cheese, lemon juice and salt and pepper to taste. Blitz until you have a smooth purée. Scoop into a bowl, top with the cornichons and scatter over the chives. To serve, snap the crispbreads into shards and use to scoop up the dip.

**For the crispbread**
200g (2 cups) rye flour
200g (¾ cup) plain (all-purpose) flour, plus extra rolling
50g (⅓ cup) nigella seeds
1 tsp fine salt
1 tsp instant yeast
300ml (1¼ cups) warm water

**For the carrot dip**
700g (25oz) carrots, peeled and cut into 1.5cm (¾ inch) discs
1 tbsp olive oil
1 heaped tsp caraway seeds, lightly crushed in a pestle and mortar
200g (1 cup) full-fat cream cheese
juice of ½–1 lemon, to taste
salt and freshly ground black pepper

**To garnish**
6 cornichons (small gherkins), chopped
a few chives, snipped

# Stuffed and wrapped

# Portobello mushrooms stuffed with borlotti beans and Taleggio

**Large meaty Portobello mushrooms are made for grilling, retaining their texture and soaking up the smoky grilled flavours. I used Taleggio cheese here as I love the flavour as well as the texture, but you could substitute any oozy, melty cheese like Brie or mozzarella if you prefer.**

**Serves 4–6**

Fire up your barbecue ready for direct grilling.

Melt the butter in a bowl in the microwave or in a small pan on the hob. Add the parsley and garlic and season with a little salt and pepper.

Twist out the stalk of each mushroom and finely chop, adding to the garlic butter. Add the borlotti beans and stir together, mashing the beans a little with the back of the spoon.

Lightly brush the mushrooms with a little olive oil and rest them, gill side down, on the grill bars of the barbecue. Shut the lid and cook for about 10 minutes, until softening and lightly coloured on the cooked side. Remove to a barbecue-proof roasting tray and shut the barbecue lid so it maintains an even oven-like temperature.

Place a piece of Taleggio in the hollow of each mushroom and top with the garlic butter and bean mixture, pressing it well into the corners. Sprinkle over a few breadcrumbs and finish with a final drizzle of oil.

Slide the tray on to the barbecue and close the lid, leaving it to cook for 10–15 minutes, until the breadcrumbs are crisp, the mushrooms tender and the cheese melting. Cooking them on a tray means that any cheese that oozes up and explodes out of the mushrooms is not lost to the barbecue.

50g (2oz) butter
a small handful of flat-leaf parsley, chopped
2 cloves of garlic, crushed
8 Portobello mushrooms
400g (14oz) can of borlotti beans (240g/8½oz drained weight), drained and rinsed
a little olive oil, for brushing and drizzling
100g (3½oz) Taleggio, cut into 8 pieces (or other melty cheese, like Brie)
25g (½ cup) fresh breadcrumbs
salt and freshly ground black pepper

# RED PEPPERS, STUFFED THREE WAYS

I make no apologies for giving three stuffed pepper recipes in a row, as they are perhaps the most quintessential of all grilling vegetables. They simply taste at their best cooked over fire or a really high heat, and they have a nice big cavity into which you can stuff all manner of tasty things. Once you've tried these three ideas, experiment to your heart's content. Two things to note: the fillings here are enough to fill largish peppers, and when you are choosing your peppers think about how they will lie once sliced in half through the stem – try to choose fairly flat-sided peppers that won't wobble about too much on the barbecue. But if they are a bit wobbly you can always roll up little logs of foil to use as 'chocks' to support them as they cook.

These recipes all cook best on a barbecue and wouldn't really work on a griddle pan. You can, however, achieve a similar charring effect by roasting them in a hot oven.

## Peppers stuffed with spiced couscous and cashew butter sauce

Cashew butter is a complete doddle to make provided you have a food processor – you just chuck in the nuts, grind them up, and over a few minutes they release their oils and turn quite magically into a smooth and creamy paste. This recipe makes about double the cashew butter you need, as it's not practical to try and make less in a processor, but it will keep for 3 months in the fridge and is delicious on toast – just use it like you would peanut butter. You could also use ready-made cashew butter if you prefer.

**Serves 3–6, depending on what else you are eating**

Begin by tipping the cashews into a large dry frying pan and setting it over a medium heat. Toast for a few minutes, tossing to mix about as the cashews cook, until they are golden in patches.

Transfer to a food processor and whizz on a high speed for a good 8–10 minutes, until you have a thick creamy paste, stopping to scrape the bowl down a few times to make sure all the nuts get completely ground up. Add some salt and whizz once more to blend – start with around a teaspoon and adjust to taste.

**For the cashew butter and coriander sauce**
250g (2 cups) unsalted cashews
1 tsp salt, or to taste
a small bunch of coriander
   (cilantro), finely chopped
a little lemon juice, to taste

**continued overleaf . . .**

Scoop about half the cashew butter into a mixing bowl and transfer the rest to a tub or jar for storing in the fridge. Add 125ml (½ cup) of cold water to the bowl and whisk vigorously until you have a smooth, creamy sauce. Add the coriander and a good squeeze of lemon juice, and a grind of black pepper if you like. Set aside.

Fire up the barbecue ready for direct and indirect grilling. If you are cooking in the oven, preheat it to 200°C fan/425°F.

Slice the peppers in half through the stem, then scrape out and discard the seeds and membranes. Lay them on a plate while you make the filling.

Put the couscous into a mixing bowl and stir in the stock powder, paprika, cinnamon and nutmeg, then pour over 325ml (1¼ cups) of boiling water, stirring well to mix. Stir in the olive oil, currants and spring onions, along with a good seasoning of salt and pepper. Divide the filling evenly between the halved peppers, pressing it well into the corners.

Carefully slide the stuffed pepper halves directly on to the grill bars, or put them into the oven on a tray, and cook until the peppers are soft and tender, about 30–40 minutes. If you are cooking over charcoal, start the peppers off indirectly so they begin to soften, then slide them directly over the heat towards the end of cooking. You may need to move the peppers around the grill a little to ensure they all cook evenly.

Drizzle a little cashew butter sauce over each pepper just before serving, and serve the rest in a bowl alongside.

**For the peppers**

3 red (bell) peppers
250g (2 cups) couscous
1 tsp good-quality vegetable stock powder
1 tsp smoked paprika
½ tsp ground cinnamon
½ tsp ground nutmeg
3 tbsp olive oil
2 tbsp currants
3 spring onions (scallions), finely chopped
salt and freshly ground black pepper

# Romano peppers stuffed with polenta, Parmesan, sage, crispy capers

Romano peppers are the long thin ones that are becoming increasingly easy to find, and although they don't taste particularly different to regular peppers they do look the business, which I always think adds a lot to the pleasure of eating. You could use regular peppers here but their thicker flesh means they will take a little more time to cook. One thing to note – the polenta will crack and shrink a little on grilling, which you may feel looks wrong, but the crispy edges are worth it, and besides, once you've doused the lot in caramelised butter, sprinkled over some extra cheese and started eating, I promise you won't give those cracks a second thought.

**Serves 3–6, depending on what else you are eating**

Slice the peppers in half through the stem, then scoop out and discard the seeds and core. Line them up on a plate or baking sheet so you can carry them easily to the barbecue.

Fire up your barbecue ready for direct or indirect grilling. If you are cooking in the oven, preheat it to 200°C fan/425°F.

Put the stock into a pan, set over a high heat and bring to the boil. Once boiling, slowly pour in the polenta, stirring constantly so no lumps form. Reduce the heat to medium-low and continue to cook, stirring all the time, until thickened – about 5 minutes. Take a little care, as it does have a tendency to spit molten bubbles. Turn off the heat and add the butter and most of the Parmesan (reserving a little for later), stirring until it's melted and smooth. Season generously with salt and pepper and spoon into the cut pepper halves, making sure it goes into the corners and crevices.

**continued overleaf . . .**

3 large Romano peppers
400ml (1¾ cups) vegetable stock
80g (½ cup) instant polenta (cornmeal)
25g (1oz) butter
50g (2oz) Parmesan, freshly grated
salt and freshly ground black pepper

**To top**
60g (2¼oz) butter
3 tbsp capers
about 12 sage leaves

Use tongs to carefully slide the peppers directly on to the grill bars, or put them into the oven on a tray. Cook for 15–20 minutes, or until the peppers are lightly charred on the base and soft to the touch and the polenta is crisping up a little on top. Start the peppers off away from the heat source until they begin to soften, then slide them directly over the fire to finish cooking. If you are grilling with gas, start with a lower flame and gradually increase the heat towards the end of cooking.

When the peppers are about halfway cooked, put the butter, capers and whole sage leaves into a heatproof skillet and rest it on the barbecue directly over the fire. Alternatively, set the pan on the hob over a medium-high heat. Cook for about 10 minutes, until the butter is lightly caramelised and the capers and sage are crisp.

To serve, transfer the peppers to a platter and pour over the butter sauce. Finish with a final grating of Parmesan and eat immediately.

# Grilled peppers with chickpeas, tomatoes, black olives and harissa yoghurt

A Mediterranean-inspired stuffed pepper, packed full of sunshine flavours. Like all three of the pepper recipes here, these are best started off over a gentle heat so the peppers can begin to soften without charring too much.

**Serves 3–6, depending on what else you are eating**

Fire up your barbecue ready for direct or indirect grilling. If you are cooking in the oven, preheat it to 200°C fan/425°F.

Slice the peppers in half through the stem, then scoop out and discard the seeds and core. Line them up on a plate or baking sheet so you can carry them easily to the barbecue.

Set a frying pan over a medium-low heat, add the oil and onion and fry for a good 15 minutes, or until softening and lightly caramelised. Transfer to a bowl and stir in the chickpeas, garlic, tomatoes, olives, sun-dried tomatoes and parsley. Season with a little salt and a good grind of pepper. Spoon the filling into the peppers, pushing it well into the corners.

Carefully transfer the stuffed peppers to the grill, or into the oven on a tray, and cook for 30–40 minutes, until the peppers are lightly charred and soft to the touch. Start them off indirectly until they begin to soften, then slide them directly above the fire to finish off chargrilling. If you are cooking over a gas barbecue, start off over a lower flame and gradually increase the heat as the peppers begin to soften.

Once the peppers are cooked, transfer them to a plate. Top each with a dollop of yoghurt, a little harissa and an extra sprinkle of parsley and serve while hot.

3 large red (bell) peppers
2 tbsp olive oil
1 large onion, finely chopped
400g (14oz) can of chickpeas, drained and rinsed
2 cloves of garlic, crushed
6 cherry tomatoes, quartered
60g (½ cup) black olives, chopped
60g (½ cup) sun-dried tomatoes, chopped
a few sprigs of flat-leaf parsley, chopped
salt and freshly ground black pepper

**To serve**
3 tbsp Greek yoghurt
3 tsp harissa
a little extra flat-leaf parsley, chopped

# Coconut aubergine, sesame noodles and chilli lime dressing

Soaking aubergine in coconut milk makes it become succulent and almost mushroomy in texture. Combined with crisp noodles, soft lettuce and a punchy dressing, this is simply an explosion of good things to eat.

**Serves 4–6**

Spread the aubergine slices in a single layer in a shallow dish and pour over the coconut milk. Sprinkle over the chilli flakes and season with a little salt and pepper. Set aside for an hour, turning regularly, until they have absorbed most of the liquid.

Meanwhile, plunge the noodles into a pan of boiling water, cook for a few minutes, until tender, and drain well. Tip them into a bowl and toss with the sesame oil and seeds. Season to taste with salt and pepper and set aside.

To make the dressing, mix everything together in a small bowl. Start with a little sugar, adding more to taste. It should have a good balance of sweet, sour, salty and sharp.

When you are ready to cook, fire up the barbecue, or preheat a cast-iron griddle on the hob.

Grill the aubergine slices on both sides for about 20–25 minutes until tender and lightly charred, basting with any leftover coconut milk as they cook. Once cooked, pile to one side of the barbecue to keep warm or transfer to a plate and cover with foil.

Set a plancha over the fire or on the hob to heat up. Once hot, use tongs to place little piles of noodles, well spaced out, on the plancha and leave to fry for about 5 minutes. They should develop a lovely golden crust – press them down a little with a fish slice to encourage browning. Flip over and fry for another 5 minutes. Don't worry if the piles of noodles are a bit straggly; the main thing is to make sure you get lots of crisp golden bits, combined with some soft inside bits.

Once the aubergines and noodles are cooked, pile a bit of both into each lettuce leaf. Sprinkle with spring onions, peanuts and a little mint and drizzle with dressing. Roll up the lettuce leaves to eat with your hands (with plenty of napkins!).

1 large aubergine (eggplant), about 350g (12oz), cut into 5mm (¼ inch) slices
200ml (1⅓ cups) coconut milk
1 tsp chilli flakes (optional)
salt and freshly ground black pepper

**For the crisp sesame noodles**
2 blocks of dried medium egg noodles
2 tsp toasted sesame oil
2 tsp sesame seeds

**For the dressing**
juice of 2 limes
3 tbsp soy sauce
2 cloves of garlic, crushed
2–3 bird's-eye chillies, finely chopped, to taste
2–3 tsp caster sugar, to taste

**To serve**
1 soft lettuce, torn into leaves
1 bunch of spring onions (scallions), thinly sliced
a good handful of salted peanuts, roughly chopped
mint leaves, roughly chopped, to garnish

# Corn on the cob, Cambodian coconut, lime and chilli baste

I just love the flavours of Cambodian cooking and this easy baste is no exception – sweet, creamy, hot and salty, a real explosion of tastes that works so well to liven up succulent grilled sweetcorn.

**Serves 4**

Fire up your barbecue ready for direct grilling, or preheat a cast-iron griddle pan on the hob. This recipe is best cooked outside on a barbecue if you can. If you cook it on a griddle, be prepared for a bit of smoke once you start brushing on the baste.

If your sweetcorn still has its husks attached, you don't need to do anything to it. If it's naked, wrap each cob in a good layer of foil. Lay the corn on the barbecue or griddle and cook for a good 20 minutes, turning regularly.

While the corn is having its initial grill, prepare the baste by mixing the rest of the ingredients together in a small bowl.

Peel back the husks on each cob, leaving them intact as they make a great handle for both turning and eating, or peel away and discard the foil. Return the corn to the barbecue or griddle and begin to brush with the coconut and lime baste. Cook for another 10–15 minutes, basting and turning frequently, until the corn is succulent and lightly charred.

Allow to cool for a few minutes before tucking in, as they will be super hot straight from the grill.

4 corn on the cob, ideally with
   husks attached
4 tbsp coconut cream
juice and zest of 1 lime
1 tbsp soy sauce
2 tsp palm sugar or soft light
   brown sugar
2 bird's-eye chillies, finely
   chopped
a couple of sprigs of mint, leaves
   finely chopped
salt and freshly ground black
   pepper

# Hasselback potatoes, salsa verde dressing

**Cutting a myriad of thin slits through new potatoes might seem like a hassle (apologies, I couldn't resist!), but I urge you to make these. Not only a brilliant way of buffing up your knife skills, but the more cuts you make, the crisper the outsides will become. On a barbecue you have the bonus of adding smoky flavours.**

**Serves about 4 as a side**

Fire up your barbecue ready for direct grilling. If you are cooking in the oven, preheat it to 200°C fan/425°F.

Place a potato on a chopping board. Cut slices three-quarters of the way through, all the way along the potato, about 2mm apart, taking care not to cut all the way through. Put into a bowl and continue with the other potatoes. Drizzle over the olive oil and season generously with salt and pepper. Toss well to mix.

Take two large sheets of foil and lay them out in a cross shape. Tip the prepared potatoes into the middle, arranging them in a single layer. Seal up the foil tight to form a parcel and place it on the grill bars. Shut the lid and leave to cook for an hour, turning over halfway. Once the potatoes are tender, carefully open the parcel and remove the potatoes one by one directly on to the hot grill bars. Cook for another 20–30 minutes, turning a few times, until they are crisp. If you are cooking in the oven, simply line up in a single layer on a tray and roast for about an hour.

For the salsa verde, put the herbs, garlic and mustard into a food processor and pulse until roughly combined. Add the capers, cornichons, lemon juice and sugar, starting with a little of each, and pulse to a paste, loosening the sauce with the olive oil. Taste as you go and add a little more of what you fancy. Season with salt and pepper.

Serve the potatoes with the salsa verde alongside.

1 kg (2lb 3oz) new potatoes, washed but not peeled
3 tbsp olive oil
salt and freshly ground black pepper

**For the salsa verde**
a generous bunch of flat-leaf parsley, roughly torn
a small bunch of mint, roughly torn
a small bunch of chives, roughly torn
1 clove of garlic, roughly chopped
1 tbsp Dijon mustard
2–3 tbsp capers
3–4 cornichons (small gherkins)
juice of ½–1 lemon
1–2 tsp caster sugar
100–150ml (⅓–⅔ cup) extra virgin olive oil
salt and freshly ground black pepper

# Grilled cauliflower 'steaks' with feta, oregano and lemon

One of my favourite things to do with cauliflower, so easy and summery. Thick juicy slices are grilled until lightly charred, then topped with feta and a Greek-inspired lemon and herb sprinkle. The cauliflower slices get part wrapped in foil so you don't lose any of the precious juices to the grill while cooking.

**Serves 4**

Fire up the barbecue ready for direct grilling.

Remove the leaves from both cauliflowers. Then place one base down on a chopping board and carefully slice off each side, about 3cm (1¼ inches) from the centre of the stem, so you are left with about a 6cm (2½ inch) wedge of cauliflower with the stem in the middle. Save the trimmings for soup or a stir-fry, including the leaves, which make for great eating.

Now carefully cut right through the centre of the stem to give you 2 thick 'steaks' of cauliflower, with the florets joined to the stem. Repeat with the other cauliflower.

Drizzle olive oil over the cauliflower slices and season well with plenty of pepper and a little salt. Lay directly on the grill bars and cook for about 20 minutes, until lightly caramelised. Slide the cauliflower slices around a few times to make sure they are all cooking evenly.

While the cauliflower is cooking on the first side, make the herby sprinkle. Mix together the oregano, garlic and lemon zest in a small bowl. Reserve the lemon for squeezing over as you serve.

Tear off 4 sheets of tin foil just a little bigger than the cauliflower slices and have them ready by the grill, along with the wedges of feta.

Use a fish slice to lift the cauliflower slices and lay each one, caramelised side up, on a piece of foil. Sprinkle over the herby

2 medium cauliflowers
1 tbsp olive oil
a small bunch of fresh oregano, leaves chopped
2 cloves of garlic, chopped
finely grated zest of 1 large lemon
2 x 200g (7oz) packs of feta, each cut in half
freshly ground black pepper

**To serve**
lemon juice
extra virgin olive oil

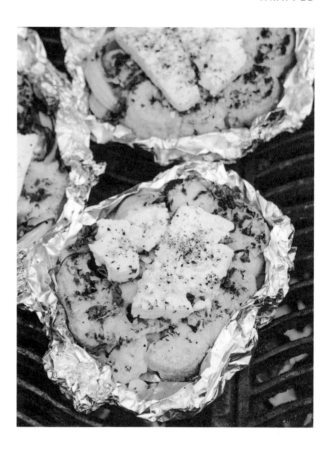

mixture and top each with a wedge of feta. Grind over a little
pepper, then scrunch up the sides of the foil to make a wall that
will keep all the cooking juices and cheese inside. Return to the
grill bars to finish cooking with the lid down for 15 minutes, or
until the cauliflower is tender when pricked with a sharp knife.

Serve immediately, with a good squeeze of lemon juice and a
drizzle of extra virgin olive oil.

# Georgian-style walnut and herb aubergine rolls

**These colourful rolls are great for a party, as you can assemble them ahead of time and serve them at room temperature, adding the garnishes just before serving.**

**Makes about 16, serving 4–6 as a snack or starter**

Fire up the barbecue ready for direct grilling, or preheat a griddle pan on the hob.

To make the walnut filling, tip the nuts into a large dry frying pan and set over a high heat to toast for a few minutes. Tip into a food processor and blitz until coarsely ground.

Add the fenugreek, coriander seeds and chilli to the same pan and toast for a few seconds until you can smell their aroma wafting up – it won't take long, as the pan will be hot. Put them into a spice mill or a pestle and mortar and grind. Add to the walnuts in the processor, along with the garlic, vinegar and boiling water. Whizz for a minute or so, until you have a smooth, spreadable paste. Season to taste with salt and pepper, then scoop into a bowl and set aside. You can also make the sauce traditionally by pounding everything in a large pestle and mortar, but be prepared to use a little elbow grease in order to form a paste.

Cut the aubergines lengthways into 5–7mm (¼ inch) slices. Brush them all over with the olive oil and season with a little salt and pepper. Spread them out over the grill bars or griddle and cook for around 12–15 minutes, turning them a few times, until completely soft and lightly charred. Cook in batches if necessary.

Once all the aubergines are cooked, spread each slice with a thin layer of walnut paste. Sprinkle over most of the pomegranate seeds and herbs, reserving a little of both to garnish. Roll up each slice and arrange on a large platter. Sprinkle over the rest of the pomegranate seeds and herbs and finish with a generous drizzle of pomegranate molasses.

200g (1¾ cups) walnuts
1 heaped tsp fenugreek seeds
1 heaped tsp coriander seeds
½ tsp chilli flakes
2 cloves of garlic, chopped
1–2 tbsp red wine vinegar, to taste
125ml (½ cup) boiling water
3 aubergines (eggplants), about 350g (12oz) each
3–4 tbsp olive oil
1 large pomegranate, seeds picked
a small bunch of coriander (cilantro), chopped
a small bunch of flat-leaf parsley, chopped
3 tbsp pomegranate molasses, or to taste
salt and freshly ground black pepper

# Lentil-stuffed courgettes, ricotta, fresh mint sauce

**This summery dish is best served at room temperature rather than hot straight from the grill, so it's handy to make ahead of time as part of a mezze spread.**

**Serves 4–6**

Tip the lentils into a sieve and rinse well under cold running water, then transfer to a pan. Cover with cold water, add the onion and bay leaves and set on the hob over a high heat. Bring to the boil, then reduce the heat to a steady simmer and cook until the lentils are tender, about 30 minutes. Drain well, tip into a bowl, add half the extra virgin olive oil and the garlic and season well with salt and pepper. Set aside.

Make the mint sauce by pouring the boiling water into a heatproof jug and stirring in the sugar and a little salt until dissolved. Add the mint and vinegar, stir well and set aside.

Fire up your barbecue ready for direct grilling.

Slice the courgettes in half lengthways, then cut small criss-cross slashes down the cut face, first in one direction, then in the other, to make a diamond pattern. This will help the heat to penetrate the courgettes. Drizzle over the olive oil and season with a little salt and pepper. Lay the courgettes face down on the grill and cook for 10 minutes, or until the flesh is soft. Transfer them to an old baking tray, cut side upwards, and leave to cool for a few minutes. Use a teaspoon to scoop out the flesh from the centre of each courgette, leaving a 5mm (¼ inch) border around the sides. Chop the flesh and stir through the lentils, then spoon this mix into the courgette shells. Rest the baking tray directly on the grill bars and shut the barbecue lid. Cook for a good 12–15 minutes, until the courgettes are soft on the underside. Remove the tray and set aside to cool to room temperature.

Once cool, carefully transfer the courgettes to a serving plate using a fish slice – they will be quite delicate. Dot the top with the ricotta and drizzle over the mint sauce and the rest of the extra virgin olive oil. Add a final grind of pepper before serving.

### For the lentil filling
150g (¾ cup) small dark green lentils (lentilles vertes or Puy lentils)
1 small onion, finely chopped
2 bay leaves
4 tbsp extra virgin olive oil
1–2 cloves of garlic, crushed
750g (1½lb) courgettes (zucchini) (about 5 medium)
1 tbsp olive oil
200g (7oz) ricotta
salt and freshly ground black pepper

### For the mint sauce
75ml (⅓ cup) boiling water
1 tbsp caster sugar
25g (1oz) mint, leaves stripped and finely chopped
75ml red wine vinegar
a little salt, to taste

# Beef tomatoes stuffed with herby bulgur wheat

**Big juicy tomatoes stuffed with a Middle Eastern-inspired filling. Wrapping foil around each tomato just helps to give them a little structural support – once cooked they will be rather prone to collapsing when you transfer them from grill to plate.**

**Serves 4 as a side dish**

Fire up your barbecue ready for direct and indirect grilling, or preheat the oven to 200°C fan/425°F.

Put the bulgur wheat into a bowl and pour over the vegetable stock, stirring briefly. Cover and set aside for 30 minutes.

Cut a 1cm (½ inch) slice off the top of each tomato, reserving the top as a lid. Use a small knife and teaspoon to cut and scoop out the flesh and seeds of each tomato. Chop the flesh and put it into a bowl, draining off most of the juice as you go. Stir in the parsley, mint, spring onions, lemon zest, garlic and bulgur wheat and season with salt and pepper. Spoon the filling into the tomatoes, pressing well down into the base, and top each one with the reserved lid. Tear off four squares of foil and place a tomato on each one, bringing the sides up and scrunching to make a wall.

Set the tomatoes on the barbecue, slightly away from the fire, then shut the lid and leave to cook for 15–20 minutes, until the tomatoes are tender. Remove the lid from each tomato and place skin side down on the grill bars over the fire to colour up a little. At the same time, slide the tomatoes directly over the fire too, so they can lightly char on the base for another 10–15 minutes or so. If you are roasting them in the oven, line them up on a tray and cook for around 30–35 minutes. You won't need to remove the tops to cook them separately.

Once cooked, leave the tomatoes to cool a little – they are best eaten warm rather than straight from the grill. Remove the lids, squeeze over the lemon juice and give each tomato a generous drizzle of olive oil before putting the lids back on and serving.

50g (¼ cup) bulgur wheat

100ml (½ cup) hot vegetable stock

4 large beef tomatoes, about 250–270g (9–10oz) each

30g (1oz) flat-leaf parsley leaves, chopped

a loose handful of mint leaves, chopped

4 spring onions (scallions), finely chopped

zest and juice of 1 lemon

1 clove of garlic, crushed

salt and freshly ground black pepper

2–3 tbsp extra virgin olive oil, to serve

# Butternut squash, stuffed with rice, wild mushrooms and Parmesan

I used rather petite butternut squash here, so that each half generously serves one. I had wanted to use those sweet little mini pumpkins that appear in the shops in the run up to Halloween, but as it turns out they are largely tasteless and sometimes impossibly tough-skinned. If you grow your own mini squash you could be in luck, or you could try a larger squash, just cooking it for longer over indirect heat before stuffing. As with all these stuffed vegetable recipes, it's rather hard to be precise about the amount of filling you might need as the available area for stuffing can vary quite a bit.

**Serves 4**

Fire up your barbecue ready for direct and indirect grilling. If you are cooking in the oven, preheat it to 200°C fan/425°F.

Slice each squash in half lengthways and scoop out and discard the seeds and membranes. Use a small sharp knife to score deeply through the flesh in a criss-cross pattern, taking care not to pierce all the way through to the skin side. Brush half the olive oil all over the squash and season the cut face with salt and pepper. Lay cut side down on your barbecue, away from the fire. Leave pretty much undisturbed for 35 minutes, so that they start to soften nicely and the underside begins to caramelise. At this stage you could chuck a handful of smoking wood chips or chunks on to the fire for some extra smoky flavours. If you are roasting them in the oven, simply place them cut side up on a tray and roast for about the same amount of time.

While the squash is cooking, prepare the filling. Measure 300ml (1¼ cups) of boiling water into a heatproof jug and stir in the dried mushrooms. Set aside to soak for a good 20 minutes, then fish them out of the jug, reserving the soaking liquid. Finely chop and add to a bowl.

**continued overleaf . . .**

2 small butternut squash, about 550–600g (19–21oz) each
2 tbsp olive oil
25g (1 cup) dried porcini mushrooms
1 red onion, finely chopped
2 cloves of garlic, crushed
100g (½ cup) mixed basmati and wild rice
2 tsp mushroom ketchup
a few sage leaves, finely chopped (or ½ tsp dried sage)
60g (2¼oz) Parmesan, freshly grated
salt and freshly ground black pepper
a handful of rocket (arugula), to serve

Pour the other half of the oil into a small frying pan and set over a medium-low heat. Once hot, add the onion and cook for about 20 minutes, or until soft and lightly caramelised. Stir in the garlic and cook for 1 more minute, then scoop into the bowl of mushrooms.

Put the rice into a small pan and pour over plenty of boiling water. Set over a high heat and boil for 5 minutes, then drain well. Tip into the bowl of mushrooms and onions and stir in the mushroom ketchup, sage and a generous two-thirds of the Parmesan, along with plenty of salt and pepper. Pour in enough of the mushroom soaking liquid to cover the rice by about 5mm (¼ inch) or so, stirring well as you go.

Once the squash have had their initial cook, turn them over so they are cut side up. Divide the rice stuffing between the halves, pressing it into the holes in the centre. If there is any liquid left in the bowl, pour that over – it's fine if it runs out of the hole and down the rest of the squash, it will just add extra flavour. Loosely cover the top of each squash half with a little foil, to create a steamy tent for the rice to finish cooking. Close the lid of the barbecue and cook for a further 30 minutes or so. Towards the end of cooking you can slide the squash a little more over the direct heat to caramelise the base.

To serve, scatter a little rocket on to 4 plates, top with the squash and grate over the rest of the Parmesan.

# Grilled chilli and cheese tamales, chocolate and ancho chilli mole

Quite an involved recipe, but worth it for the complex and unusual flavours. However, you can make everything a couple of days ahead, so then it becomes very easy when you want to grill them. You can also freeze both the steamed tamales and the mole, defrosting before grilling.

**Makes 12 tamales, serving 4–6**

Make the tamale filling first. Heat up a griddle over a high heat and, once hot, lay in the chillies. Cook for about 10–15 minutes, turning them regularly, until charred all over. Remove to a bowl, cover with clingfilm and leave to cool. Peel, deseed and roughly chop the flesh, putting it into a small bowl as you go. Stir in the feta and coriander and set aside.

Put the masa harina into a mixing bowl and stir in the baking powder and salt. Add the melted butter and the stock, stirring constantly until you have a smooth, pliable dough. Knead briefly to make sure it's evenly mixed, then divide into 12 even pieces, rolling each into a ball as you go.

To assemble the tamales, spread out 12 of the rehydrated corn husks on the worktop and put one of the balls of masa dough in the centre of each. Use your hands to flatten out the dough so it covers the husk in a rough rectangle about 4–5mm (¼ inch) thick, ensuring you have a generous 2.5cm (1 inch) border of uncovered husk all round. The thinner you can get the masa the better, as it swells on cooking.

Place a little line of the chilli and feta filling down the centre of each masa dough rectangle. Roll up the sides over the filling, drawing the masa dough together at the top so you have a sausage shape of dough with a line of filling down the inside. Roll the sides up and tuck in the ends to form a neat parcel, resting them seam side down as you go. Tear the remaining husks into 1cm (½ inch) wide strips. Use 2 or 3 of these per parcel to tie around the folded ends to secure.

**continued overleaf . . .**

## For the tamales

12 jalapeño chillies (or other green chillies if jalapeños are unavailable)
100g (3½oz) feta, crumbled
30g (2 cups) coriander (cilantro), chopped
300g (2 cups) masa harina
2 tsp baking powder
½ tsp fine salt
75g (3oz) butter, melted
about 300ml (1¼ cups) hot vegetable stock
salt and freshly ground black pepper

## For the chocolate and ancho chilli mole

3 dried ancho chillies, stalks removed
2 tbsp raisins
25g (¼ cup) pumpkin seeds
1 tsp cumin seeds
1 tsp coriander seeds
½ tsp ground cinnamon
1 tbsp olive oil
1 onion, chopped
3 cloves of garlic, chopped
25g (1oz) dark chocolate (70%)

## You also need

15 dry corn husks, soaked for an hour in boiling water, then drained

Stack the tamales end down in a large steamer basket. Pour
boiling water into the pan to just under the level of the steamer
and set over a medium heat. Cover with a tight-fitting lid and
steam for 30 minutes, checking the level of the water every now
and then and topping up as necessary. Remove from the steamer
and set aside until you are ready to grill.

While the tamales are steaming, make the mole. Put the chillies
and raisins into a jug and pour over 400ml (1¾ cups) of boiling
water to cover. Set aside.

Set a small pan over a high heat and tip in the pumpkin seeds,
allowing them to toast for a few minutes until the skin starts to
crackle and pop. Transfer to a bowl and set aside. Add the spices
to the pan and toast for just a few seconds, then tip them into a
pestle and mortar and roughly grind. Set aside.

Pour the oil into the pan, set back over a low heat and add the
onion. Fry gently for about 20 minutes until soft, then stir in the
garlic and fry for just another minute. Hang a sieve over the pan
and pour in the chilli and raisin soaking liquid. Tip the drained
chillies and raisins on to a chopping board and roughly chop,
then add them to the pan. Add the pumpkin seeds and ground
spices, bring to the boil, then reduce the heat to a simmer. Cook
for 10 minutes to soften the seeds, then stir in the chocolate until
it melts. Use a stick blender in the pan to purée everything until
smooth. Pour into a serving bowl and leave to cool.

When you are ready to eat, fire up the barbecue ready for direct
grilling, or preheat a griddle pan on the hob. Once hot, lay on the
tamales and cook for around 15 minutes, until charred all over.

To serve, unwrap, place on serving plates and spoon over a little
of the mole before eating.

# Charred leek vinaigrette, crumbled eggs, walnuts

Charring the leeks adds an extra flavour dimension and the walnuts add some welcome nuggets of crunch in this classic salad dish. Even the most tenderly cooked leeks can be tricky to slice on the plate – my best advice is to follow the grain of the leaves, slice down the length of the leek, and twirl them up on your fork like spaghetti.

**Serves 4 as a starter or side dish**

Fire up the barbecue ready for direct grilling, or, if you have a large enough griddle, preheat it on the hob.

Slice the leeks lengthways almost to the root, but leaving about 3-4cm (1¼-1½ inches) intact so the leaves stay together. Turn and cut through again on the other side, so your leek is slashed into quarters, all attached at the root end. Wash them really well under running water to remove any mud and grit, and shake to dry. Spread out on a baking sheet and drizzle over the oil, using your hands to spread it all over the leeks from top to bottom and in between the leaves so they are thinly coated all over. Season with a little salt and pepper and take to the barbecue.

Lay the leeks directly on the grill bars, and grill for 10 minutes, until charred at the edges, turning a couple of times. Take a large sheet of foil and lift the leeks on to it, then wrap the foil round them to make a parcel. Lay the parcel back over the fire and cook for another 10 minutes, turning once. Remove the parcel to a tray and leave to cool.

To make the dressing, place the red wine vinegar, mustard, caster sugar and most of the chives (save a few to garnish) in a mixing bowl. Season well with salt and pepper and whisk together thoroughly. Gradually whisk in the oil so the dressing emulsifies. Check the seasoning, whisking through just a splash more vinegar if you want to sharpen it and adding more salt, pepper or a pinch of sugar to taste.

To serve, unwrap the parcel and place one leek on each plate, separating the leaves. Drizzle over a little of the dressing. Sprinkle over the chopped egg, along with the walnuts, reserved chives and a grind of black pepper.

4 slender leeks, trimmed (about 3cm/1¼ inches in diameter)
1 tbsp olive oil
2 eggs, hard-boiled, peeled and chopped
salt and freshly ground black pepper

**For the vinaigrette**
3 tbsp red wine vinegar
2 tbsp Dijon mustard
2 tsp caster sugar
a small bunch of chives, snipped
100ml (⅓ cup) extra virgin olive oil

**To garnish**
25g (¼ cup) walnuts, toasted and chopped

# Cheese and chilli stuffed jalapeños

**The ideal snack to accompany a really cold beer? I certainly think so . . . The trick to these is to choose the biggest, fattest chillies you can find as you get more room for melty, spicy cheese. When I can't find true jalapeños I make these with the large green chillies you can find in Asian stores. Ideally, cook these on a plancha on the barbecue so any cheese that oozes from the chillies as they grill can turn into delectable crunchy bits.**

**Serves about 4 as a bar snack**

Fire up your barbecue ready for direct grilling, ideally resting a plancha on the grill bars to heat up.

While the grill is coming up to temperature, slice the chillies in half lengthways through the stalk. Scoop out and discard the membranes and seeds.

Mix together the mozzarella, Cheddar, cumin and smoked paprika in a bowl, seasoning to taste with salt and pepper. Spoon this mixture into the chilli halves, pressing it well into the corners and crevices.

Once the plancha is hot, lightly brush it with just a little oil, then lay on the stuffed chillies and close the barbecue lid. Cook for about 10 minutes, or until the cheese is molten and the chillies are soft and nicely charred underneath.

Leave to cool for just enough time to prevent you burning your mouth, then tuck in!

250–300g (9–10oz) jalapeños (ideally big fat ones)
125g (4oz) mozzarella, finely chopped
80g (3oz) extra mature Cheddar, grated
2 tsp cumin seeds, toasted and ground
½ tsp smoked paprika
salt and freshly ground black pepper
a little vegetable oil, for oiling

# Gozleme – stuffed flatbreads with feta and spinach

These stuffed breads make a great snack or starter, or try them with the tarator with grilled peppers and beans on page 151 for a hearty lunch. Using yoghurt in the dough makes it lovely and soft and a pleasure to knead and roll.

**Makes 6**

Put the flour, yeast and salt into a mixing bowl and stir together. Measure the boiling water into a jug and add the yoghurt, stirring until combined. Pour into the flour, stirring as you go until you have a soft dough. Tip on to a lightly floured worktop and knead until smooth.

Divide into 6 even-sized pieces, rolling each into a ball, then place on a lightly floured baking sheet. Cover with a clean tea towel and leave to prove until doubled in size – this will take about an hour at room temperature.

Meanwhile, make the filling. Roughly chop the spinach and put it into a mixing bowl. Add the cheese, grated onion and yoghurt and stir together. Tip the pine nuts into a small frying pan and set over a medium heat. Toast for a minute or two, until golden, then tip into the filling. Season generously with the nutmeg, salt and pepper.

When you are ready to cook, fire up your barbecue ready for direct grilling, or preheat a cast-iron griddle on the hob.

Dust the worktop with a little flour and roll one ball of dough out to a thin, roughly circular shape, turning it over once or twice as you roll to make sure it's not sticking to the worktop or the rolling pin. It should be a few millimetres (¼ inch or so) thick and about 25–28cm (10–11 inches) in diameter.

Fold the top of the circle over about 3–4cm (1¼–1½ inches) to straighten the top edge. Repeat with the bottom edge. Spoon 2–3 generous tablespoons of filling into the centre, and spread it out to form a rectangle around 12cm (4¾ inches) wide, avoiding the folded edges at the top and bottom. Bring one of the unfolded sides of the dough over the filling, pressing it down on the top and bottom to seal, then bring the other side

## For the dough

500g (3½ cups) plain (all-purpose) flour, plus extra for rolling
1 tsp instant yeast
½ tsp salt
100ml (⅓ cup) boiling water
300g (1½ cups) natural yoghurt

## For the filling

260g (9½oz) baby leaf spinach, washed and dried in a salad spinner
200g (7oz) feta, crumbled
1 small onion, grated
3 tbsp natural yoghurt
50g (½ cup) pine nuts
½ nutmeg, freshly grated
salt and freshly ground black pepper

over that, again pressing down to seal. Turn over so the folds are
facing down and lay on a liberally floured baking sheet. Repeat
with the other pieces of dough, spacing them out over two
baking sheets to keep them separate.

Place the gozleme directly on to the hot grill bars or griddle and
cook for about 2–3 minutes on each side, until the bread is crisp
and dark in places.

Serve immediately, but take a little care with your first bite as the
filling will be very hot.

**pictured overleaf . . .**

# Sharing plates

# Herby sweet potato wedges, lemon tahini, watercress

I love cooking sweet potatoes on a barbecue plancha, as you can add a little extra smoky flavour with some wood chips, but they also cook brilliantly on a griddle plate on the hob. Here the sweetness of the potatoes, which seems to intensify when grilled, is offset by a sharp lemony dressing and lots of peppery watercress.

**Serves 4–6 as a side dish**

Fire up your barbecue for direct grilling, setting a plancha on the grill bars, or put a cast-iron griddle pan on the hob. Leave to get really hot. Test the temperature by flicking over a few drops of water – they should sizzle instantly on impact.

Give the sweet potatoes a good scrub under running water, then chop into wedges about 2cm (¾ inch) thick. Tip them into a bowl and toss with the olive oil, oregano and smoked paprika and season well with salt and pepper.

Once the plancha or griddle is hot, tip on the seasoned sweet potatoes and spread them out in a single layer. Allow them to cook until crisp on the outside and tender inside, about 30 minutes or so, flipping over a few times to make sure they are cooking evenly. Add a few smoking wood chunks or chips as they cook if you like.

While the sweet potatoes are cooking, make the lemon tahini dressing. Put the tahini, lemon zest and juice, garlic and 50–75ml (¼ cup) of cold water into a deep jug. Use a stick blender to pulse to a smooth dressing, adding a little more water if necessary. Season to taste with salt and pepper. Alternatively, crush the garlic until smooth, then whisk everything together in a bowl.

To serve, scatter the watercress over a platter and tip over the sweet potato wedges. Drizzle on the dressing and serve immediately.

1kg (2lb 3oz) sweet potatoes
2 tbsp olive oil
1 tsp dried oregano
1 tsp smoked paprika
salt and freshly ground black pepper
2 x 100g bags of watercress (4 cups), to serve

### For the lemon tahini dressing

50g (¼ cup) tahini
zest and juice of 1 lemon
1 clove of garlic, roughly chopped

# Charred apple and kale, dolcelatte, fennel croutons

The best salads are an explosion of colours, tastes and textures, and this ticks all those boxes with ease. Perfect for those early autumn days when it's still warm enough for salad, perhaps even to eat in the garden if you are lucky. There is a little bit of prep to do here, mixing and tossing everything in different bowls before you even think about cooking, but once you get to the grill it's a pretty quick job.

**Serves about 4–6**

Make the dressing by whisking together the citrus juices and the mustard. Gradually pour in the olive oil, whisking all the time until it has emulsified. Season to taste with salt and pepper and set aside.

Preheat your barbecue ready for direct grilling, or preheat a griddle on the hob.

Put the torn bread into a bowl, drizzle in half the oil, add the crushed fennel seeds and the chilli flakes, if using, and season with a little salt and pepper. Toss to mix and set aside.

Slice the apples into 8 wedges each, removing the core. Put into a bowl, drizzle over the rest of the olive oil and add a grind of salt and pepper, tossing well until coated.

Give the cavolo nero a good wash under running water and shake dry. You need to remove the tough central stem of each leaf. The easiest way to do this is to take a leaf and grasp it firmly at the base end. Use your other hand to wrap around the leaf and swoosh up the stem in one swift motion, keeping hold of the stem firmly as you go. You should be left with both sides of the leaf still attached at the tip. Tear into large bite-sized pieces and toss them with the apples in the bowl.

Depending on the size of your barbecue or griddle, you may need to grill everything separately – there is quite a volume to cook. Start with the apple wedges, cooking them for a couple of minutes each side until they are lightly caramelised and starting to soften a little. Transfer to a plate. Then spread out

## For the dressing
juice of ½ orange
juice of ½ lemon
1 tbsp Dijon mustard
3 tbsp extra virgin olive oil
salt and freshly-ground black
    pepper

## For the salad
150g (5oz) ciabatta or sourdough
    (a couple of slices), torn into
    bite-sized pieces
3 tbsp olive oil
1 tbsp fennel seeds, crushed in a
    pestle and mortar
½ tsp dried chilli flakes
    (optional)
4 medium dessert apples
300g (10½oz) cavolo nero
150g (5oz) dolcelatte, cut into
    roughly 2cm (¾ inch) cubes

the cavolo nero across the grill, cooking for a couple of minutes each side, pressing down with tongs as it cooks so the leaves have maximum contact with the grill. Once cooked, transfer the leaves to the salad dressing and toss well to mix. Finally, cook the croutons for a few minutes, turning regularly, until they are crisp and golden.

Spread the dressed cavolo nero on a large plate, tucking the apple wedges in and around. Scatter over the croutons and dolcelatte and tuck in.

# Watermelon, halloumi, lime-pickled red onions

OK, I'll admit that no actual vegetables were grilled in the making of this salad but I hope you agree it is worthy of inclusion. And, after all, grilled halloumi with almost anything is very much worth eating. You can grill watermelon (useful to know if your melon is a little underripe), but I do prefer its texture when eaten raw.

**Serves 6–8**

Put the onion into a small bowl with the lime zest and juice and the sugar, stirring until the sugar has dissolved. Set aside for about 30 minutes while you prepare the rest of the salad.

Cut the watermelon into 1cm (½ inch) thick wedges, trimming off the rind as you go. Spread over a large platter.

Fire up your barbecue ready for direct grilling, or heat up a griddle pan on the hob.

Drizzle a little of the oil over the halloumi (save the rest for the salad), then place directly over the heat on the grill bars. Cook for 2–3 minutes, until seared, then turn over with a fish slice and cook the other side. Once the halloumi is cooked, cut each slice in half on the diagonal and scatter over the watermelon.

Sprinkle over the coriander, mint and pickled onion slices, drizzling over the lime juice from the bowl too. Scatter the chopped pistachios over the salad. Finish with a generous drizzle of olive oil and a grind of salt and pepper and serve immediately, while the halloumi is still warm.

1 small red onion, very thinly sliced
zest and juice of 2 limes
2 tsp caster sugar
1kg (2lb 3oz) watermelon, about ½ medium-sized one
4 tbsp olive oil
3 x 250g (9oz) blocks of halloumi, cut into 1cm (½ inch) thick slices
a small bunch of coriander (cilantro), leaves roughly chopped
a small bunch of mint, leaves roughly chopped
50g (½ cup) pistachios, toasted and roughly chopped
salt and freshly ground black pepper

# Grilled little gems, pesto, caramelised pine nuts

**Grilling lettuce sounds unusual but it really works. Cooked briefly over a high heat, it takes on lots of lovely caramelised flavours and becomes somehow more of a substantial vegetable than a salad leaf. Try it.**

**Serves 4–6 as a side dish**

Fire up your barbecue ready for direct grilling, or set a cast-iron griddle pan on the hob to heat up.

To make the pesto, put the basil into a food processor and whizz to chop. Add the tomatoes, garlic, Parmesan, olive oil and lemon juice and blend until smooth. Season to taste with salt and pepper. If you don't have a food processor, you can use a deep jug with a stick blender, or just chop everything really finely and mix together for a slightly chunkier pesto.

Set a small frying pan over a medium-high heat and add the pine nuts, sugar and smoked paprika. As the sugar begins to melt, stir to coat the nuts evenly, cooking for a few minutes until they are golden and caramelised. Transfer to a dish to cool.

When you are ready to cook, brush the lettuce generously all over with some of the dressing, working it into the layers on the cut sides. Place on the grill and cook for a few minutes, until softening and lightly charred, turning regularly.

To serve, transfer the lettuce wedges to a plate, spooning over the rest of the dressing, and sprinkle over the caramelised pine nuts. Tuck in while the lettuce wedges are still hot.

4 little gem lettuces, sliced into quarters through the root

**For the pesto dressing**
2 big bunches of basil, tough stalks trimmed
4 cherry tomatoes, chopped
1 clove of garlic, roughly chopped
50g (2oz) Parmesan, finely grated
100ml (⅓ cup) olive oil
juice of ½–1 lemon, to taste
salt and freshly ground black pepper

**For the pine nuts**
75g (⅔ cup) pine nuts
1 heaped tsp caster sugar
½ tsp smoked paprika

# Barbecued carrot, ricotta and toasted pecans

I adore this salad and would eat the whole thing myself given half a chance – the combination of sweet charred carrots, creamy ricotta and crunchy nuts is quite simply addictive. If you've never grilled a carrot before, do it now. They are an absolute revelation and show just how good fire-cooked vegetables can be.

**Serves 4–6 as a side dish**

Trim the tops off the carrots and scrub under running water. Slice in half lengthways, or into quarters if they are a little larger – you want them to be approximately finger-thickness.

Fill a pan with boiling water and add a little salt, then set over a high heat and bring back to the boil. Once boiling, add the carrots and blanch for 3 minutes. Drain well and tip into a mixing bowl. While they are still hot, add the olive oil, cumin, brown sugar, chilli flakes and garlic and stir well to mix. Cover and leave to marinate for a couple of hours at room temperature.

Once you are ready to cook, fire up your barbecue ready for direct grilling, or preheat a cast-iron griddle pan on the hob.

Lay the carrots on the grill bars or griddle and cook for 15–20 minutes, turning regularly, until they are nicely caramelised. If you are barbecuing, you can add a few smoking wood chunks or chips to up the smokiness. Use a brush to baste the carrots with any excess marinade from the bowl as you turn them.

Once soft and caramelised, scatter the carrots over a serving plate and dot with heaped teaspoons of ricotta. Sprinkle over the spring onions, chopped pecans and coriander. Finally, add a generous drizzle of olive oil and finish with a good grind of pepper. Serve while still warm.

1 x 500g (1lb 2oz) bunch of carrots, preferably with the tops on
2 tbsp olive oil
1 tbsp cumin seeds, lightly crushed in a pestle and mortar
1 tsp soft dark brown sugar
1 tsp dried chilli flakes, ideally chipotle chilli flakes
1 clove of garlic, crushed
250g (1¼ cups) ricotta
½ bunch of spring onions (scallions), thinly sliced
50g (½ cup) pecans, toasted and chopped
a small bunch of coriander (cilantro), chopped
extra virgin olive oil, to drizzle
salt and freshly ground black pepper

# Charred asparagus, pak choy and spring onions, ginger dressing, toasted cashews

**A big plateful of delicious grilled greens with a punchy ginger dressing. Just add a bowlful of steamed rice for a simple supper, or try it served alongside one of the Asian-inspired recipes in the kebab chapter.**

**Serves 2 as a main course, 4 as a side**

Fire up your barbecue ready for direct grilling, or preheat a griddle on the hob.

Trim the asparagus and spread out in a shallow tray. Slice the pak choy into 4 or 6 wedges (depending on size), cutting through the root so the pieces stay intact, and add them to the asparagus. Slice the spring onions in half lengthways and add to the tray. Drizzle over the oil, season with a little salt and pepper and toss to coat.

Spread out the veg on the grill or griddle and cook for 10 minutes, or until lightly charred and just tender, turning regularly and moving them around the grill so they cook evenly.

While the vegetables are grilling, make the dressing. Pour the sesame oil into a barbecue-proof pan, or set a frying pan on the hob if you are cooking inside. Add the ginger, garlic and chillies and gently fry for a few minutes to soften. Stir in the soy sauce and honey and once it's melted remove from the heat.

Set another pan on the barbecue or hob and add the cashews, toasting for a few minutes until golden. Tip on to a board and roughly chop.

To serve, scatter the charred vegetables over a serving plate. Pour on the warm dressing and sprinkle over the cashews.

250g (9oz) asparagus
200g (7oz) pak choy
1 bunch of spring onions (scallions)
1 tbsp vegetable oil
50g (⅓ cup) cashews
salt and freshly ground black pepper

**For the dressing**
3 tbsp sesame oil
40g (1½oz) fresh root ginger, cut into matchsticks
3 cloves of garlic, thinly sliced
2 red chillies, cut into matchsticks
4 tbsp soy sauce
1 tbsp honey

# Walnut and tarragon tarator, grilled peppers and beans

Tarator is a rich walnut and garlic sauce from Turkey that has a similar texture to hummus. Here I've flavoured it with non-traditional tarragon, as it has such a natural affinity with walnuts. This makes a colourful lunch or sharing starter when served with crusty bread for scooping up the sauce. If you are barbecuing, a flat cast-iron plancha can be used to stop the veg falling through the grill bars.

**Serves 4 as a side dish**

Fire up your barbecue ready for direct grilling, setting a plancha on the grill bars if you are using one, or preheat a cast-iron griddle on the hob.

Put the walnuts into a flameproof frying pan and rest it on the grill bars for a few minutes until lightly toasted. At the same time, lay the bread directly on the grill bars and toast lightly. If you are cooking inside, toast the nuts in a dry frying pan and the bread on the griddle.

Tip the toasted walnuts into a food processor, then tear up the bread and add that too. Whizz to coarse crumbs, then add the tarragon, garlic, olive oil and vinegar, along with a generous seasoning of salt and pepper. Blitz to a thick paste, then, with the motor running, slowly pour in enough cold water to thin the sauce to a spreadable hummus consistency. Taste to check the seasoning, adding a little more vinegar if it needs sharpening a touch. Scoop on to a serving platter and spread out.

Put the peppers and green beans into a mixing bowl and drizzle in a little oil, seasoning with salt and pepper. Toss to mix, then spread out over the plancha or griddle. Cook for about 15 minutes, turning regularly, until lightly charred.

Once the vegetables are cooked, scatter them over the plate of tarator. Sprinkle a little sumac over the top, along with a drizzle of olive oil and a little salt and pepper. Serve while warm.

3 large red (bell) peppers, sliced into 1cm (½ inch) strips
300g (10½oz) green beans, topped and tailed
1 tbsp olive oil
sumac, to sprinkle

**For the tarator sauce**
150g (1 cup) walnut halves, toasted
1 slice of white bread (about 75g/3oz)
10g (½ cup) tarragon, leaves picked
2 cloves of garlic, peeled and roughly chopped
4 tbsp extra virgin olive oil, plus extra for drizzling
2 tbsp white wine vinegar
about 175ml (¾ cup) water
salt and freshly ground black pepper

# Miso-grilled aubergine, sticky pumpkin seeds

Packed full of salty, umami flavours thanks to the miso and soy, these grilled aubergines are addictive. Sichimi togarashi is a Japanese seven-spice mix that can be sprinkled over for a chilli kick. It is well worth seeking out if you enjoy a bit of heat in your food.

**Serves 4–6**

Make the miso marinade by spooning the miso paste into a mixing bowl and gradually whisking in the soy sauce, followed by the rice vinegar, sesame oil, ginger and garlic. Remove about half to a small bowl and reserve to use as a dressing for the salad.

Slice the aubergines into chunky wedges, adding them to the marinade as you go. Toss well to mix, and set aside for a good 30 minutes to an hour to soak up the marinade.

While the aubergines are soaking, tip the pumpkin seeds into a pan along with the soy sauce and honey and set over a medium heat. Toast for a few minutes until sticky and caramelised, stirring constantly. Tip into a bowl to cool and set aside.

Fire up the barbecue ready for direct grilling, or preheat a griddle pan on the hob. Once hot, grill the aubergine wedges for 25–30 minutes, turning them and basting with any leftover marinade as you go. If they are starting to burn a little on the outside before the centre is squishy, move them to a cooler part of the grill or reduce the heat under the griddle pan. There is little worse than eating a tough aubergine!

When the aubergines are cooked, scatter the kale leaves on a serving plate and drizzle over the reserved miso dressing. Top with the hot aubergine slices and sprinkle over the spring onions and sticky toasted pumpkin seeds. Finish with a generous sprinkle of sichimi togarashi and serve immediately.

3 tbsp miso paste
3 tbsp soy sauce
3 tbsp rice vinegar
2 tbsp sesame oil
5cm (2 inch) piece of fresh root ginger, finely grated
2 cloves of garlic, crushed
2 large aubergines (eggplants)
100g (3½oz) baby kale leaves
1 bunch of spring onions (scallions), thinly sliced
sichimi togarashi flakes, to garnish

**For the sticky pumpkin seeds**
50g (⅓ cup) pumpkin seeds
1 tbsp soy sauce
1 tbsp honey

# Garlicky courgettes with lemon and Aleppo pepper

An incredibly quick and easy side dish, perfect for using up a glut of courgettes in midsummer. Aleppo pepper, also known as pul biber, is a type of dried chilli flakes that is widely used in Middle Eastern cooking, adding a splash of colour and a rich, fruity flavour with just a hint of heat. Cook the courgettes hot and fast; make sure your barbecue or griddle is at a really hot temperature so you can chargrill the outside without them becoming too soft and squishy in the middle.

**Serves 4–6**

Fire up your barbecue ready for direct grilling, or heat up a griddle pan on the hob until it's really hot.

Once you are ready to cook, toss the courgettes in a bowl with the olive oil, garlic and a little salt and pepper. Lay the courgette wedges on the grill bars and cook for about 5 minutes, until lightly charred on the underside. Turn the courgettes over and baste them with any garlic oil left in the bowl. Keep turning and basting for another 5 minutes or so while they finish cooking.

Pile the courgettes on a serving plate, squeeze over the lemon juice and sprinkle with the Aleppo pepper. Finish with a little drizzle of best-quality extra virgin olive oil and either serve while hot or leave to cool to room temperature.

4 large courgettes (zucchini), quartered lengthways and cut into wedges
3 tbsp olive oil
2 cloves of garlic, crushed
salt and freshly ground black pepper

**To serve**
1 lemon, cut into quarters
2 tsp Aleppo pepper flakes, or more to taste
a little extra virgin olive oil, for drizzling

# Oyster mushrooms and baby corn with satay sauce

I wanted to make this recipe as traditional satay skewers, but baby corn, being rather brittle and delicate, can't be poked on to a kebab stick very successfully. It cooks just as well without skewers, although if your barbecue has big gaps between the grill bars you may want to use a plancha to prevent anything sliding into the fire, or cook it on a griddle inside, where it will be equally delicious.

**Serves 4–6**

Tip the toasted coriander seeds into a pestle and mortar or a spice mill and roughly grind, then tip into a large bowl. Add the turmeric, keçap manis, soy sauce, vegetable oil, chilli and garlic, stirring well. Add the mushrooms and baby corn and gently toss together to mix. Set aside to marinate for 30 minutes to an hour at room temperature.

While the veg are marinating, make the satay sauce. Put the oil, shallots, garlic, ginger and lemongrass into a small pan and set over a medium heat, frying gently for about 10 minutes. Tip in the chopped peanuts and creamed coconut, pour in 250ml (1 cup) of water and add the soy sauce and sugar. Bring to the boil, then simmer steadily, stirring often, for 5 minutes, until the sauce has thickened a little. Use a stick blender to purée to a smoothish sauce (or leave a bit chunky if you prefer) and season to taste with a little salt and pepper.

Fire up your barbecue ready for direct grilling, adding a plancha if you have one, or preheat a griddle pan on the hob.

Spread out the mushrooms and baby corn on the barbecue or griddle and cook for about 15 minutes, turning regularly, until tender and golden brown.

To serve, pile the cooked vegetables on to a serving platter and nestle the bowl of satay sauce in the centre. Tuck in the lime wedges and sprinkle over the coriander and extra chilli, if using.

2 tbsp coriander seeds, toasted
2 tsp ground turmeric
4 tbsp keçap manis (sweet soy sauce)
3 tbsp soy sauce
1 tbsp vegetable oil
3–4 bird's-eye chillies, finely chopped, to taste
3 cloves of garlic, crushed
500g (1lb 2oz) oyster mushrooms
2 x 175g (6oz) packs of baby corn

### For the satay sauce

1 tbsp vegetable oil
2 banana shallots, finely chopped
2 cloves of garlic, crushed
2.5cm (1 inch) piece of fresh root ginger, finely grated
1 stalk of lemongrass, outer leaves discarded, inner core finely chopped
100g (3½oz) roasted salted peanuts, chopped
100g (3½oz) creamed coconut, roughly chopped
2 tbsp soy sauce
1–2 tsp soft dark brown sugar, to taste
salt and freshly ground black pepper

### To serve

1 fat lime, cut into wedges
a small bunch of coriander (cilantro), chopped
1–2 bird's-eye chillies, finely chopped (optional)

# Grilled okra with Caribbean-spiced crumbs

I have sometimes found it hard to understand the charms of okra, or lady's fingers, finding them a bit weird and often just a touch slimy. Then I decided to chuck a few on the barbecue to see what happened . . . and this is it, a very fine way to eat them indeed. The Caribbean-spiced crumbs add plenty of crunch and a lip-tingling hit of chilli that adds up to a rather winning combination. This is a great side dish to the jerk plantain kebabs on page 24.

**Serves 4–6**

Preheat the barbecue ready for direct grilling, or set a griddle pan on the hob to heat up.

Start with the spiced crumbs. Set a frying pan over a medium heat on the hob or directly on the barbecue grill bars. Pour in the olive oil and add the chillies, allspice, cinnamon, ginger, garlic, and a little salt and pepper. Stir-fry for a couple of minutes, then tip in the breadcrumbs and fry for another few minutes until they are crisp and golden, stirring frequently. Scoop into a bowl and set aside.

Put the okra into a bowl and add the olive oil and a sprinkle of sea salt flakes, tossing well to mix together. Spread on the hot barbecue, laying them perpendicular to the bars so they don't fall through, or spread them out on the griddle pan. Cook for a couple of minutes each side, so they are tender and lightly charred in places. Pile on to a serving plate and scatter over the spiced crumbs.

300g (10½oz) okra
1 tsp olive oil
sea salt flakes

**For the spiced crumbs**
2 tbsp olive oil
1–2 Scotch bonnet chillies, seeds removed, flesh very finely chopped, to taste
1 tsp ground allspice
½ tsp ground cinnamon
1cm (½ inch) slice of fresh root ginger, finely grated
1 clove of garlic, crushed
100g (2 cups) breadcrumbs (slightly stale sourdough, whizzed in a food processor, is ideal)
salt and freshly ground black pepper

# Grilled radicchio with burrata, figs and hazelnuts

Radicchio is a relative of chicory and has a similarly bitter taste that works brilliantly when paired with something sweet, like the juicy figs and creamy burrata in this recipe. Burrata is a sort of super-creamy mozzarella that's becoming increasingly easy to find in supermarkets, but you can substitute regular mozzarella if you can't get hold of any. This is such an easy but impressive salad – once you've grilled the radicchio it's basically an assembly job. With such simple ingredients you really do need to treat yourself to some good thick, sweet balsamic and top notch olive oil.

**Serves 4 as a generous starter**

Light the barbecue ready for direct grilling, or preheat a griddle pan on the hob.

Spread out the wedges of radicchio on a baking sheet, drizzle with olive oil and season well with salt and pepper. Once your barbecue or griddle is hot, lay the wedges oil side down and cook for a couple of minutes each side. Transfer to a plate.

Toast the hazelnuts in a small skillet for a few minutes, then tip on to a board and chop.

To assemble the salad, put the fig quarters and the grilled radicchio wedges on a platter. Nestle the burrata on top and sprinkle over the basil and hazelnuts. Finish with a generous drizzle of extra virgin olive oil and balsamic vinegar, add a grind of black pepper and a sprinkle of salt and serve immediately while the radicchio is still just a touch warm.

1 large head of radicchio (about 400–450g/14–16oz), sliced into 12 wedges through the root
2 tbsp olive oil
50g (½ cup) hazelnuts
4 large ripe figs, quartered
4 x 100g (3½oz) balls of burrata
a handful of basil leaves, roughly torn
3 tbsp extra virgin olive oil
2 tbsp balsamic vinegar
salt and freshly ground black pepper

# Purple sprouting with sweet garlic and chilli dressing

Purple sprouting broccoli is just great cooked on a grill, charring beautifully, although you do need to blanch it briefly to soften the stems. There is plenty of garlic in this chilli-spiked dressing, but the heat from the grill mellows the flavour so it becomes sweet rather than overwhelming.

**Serves 4–6 as a side dish**

Fire up your barbecue ready for direct grilling, or preheat a cast-iron griddle on the hob over a high heat.

Begin with the dressing. Rest the garlic cloves, whole and unpeeled, on the grill bars of the barbecue or on the griddle. Allow to soften and deeply char for about 15 minutes, turning regularly. Add the chillies alongside the garlic and grill for about 10 minutes, turning regularly, until the skin has blackened all over. Once the chillies are cooked, put them into a small bowl and cover with clingfilm so the skins loosen as they cool.

Remove the grilled garlic to a board, then peel and discard the skin and mash the flesh with the flat of a large knife. Transfer to a bowl and add the lemon juice, sugar and a good grind of salt and pepper. Whisk together until combined, then drizzle in the oil, whisking all the time until the dressing has emulsified. Peel the blackened skin from the chillies, slice them in half and scrape out and discard the seeds. Coarsely chop the flesh and stir through the dressing.

Bring a large pan of lightly salted water to the boil. Once boiling, add the purple sprouting broccoli and blanch for 2 minutes. Drain well, then transfer to a bowl, drizzle with oil and season with a little salt and pepper, tossing to mix.

Spread the broccoli over the grill or griddle and cook for about 8–10 minutes, turning regularly, until lightly charred in places. Transfer to a serving plate and drizzle over the dressing. Serve while still warm.

400g (14oz) purple sprouting broccoli
1 tbsp olive oil

**For the grilled garlic dressing**
8 fat cloves of garlic, unpeeled
4 long red chillies (medium-hot)
juice of 1 lemon
2 tsp soft brown sugar
5 tbsp (1/3 cup) olive oil
salt and freshly ground black pepper

# Chargrilled beans and mangetout with gochugaru dipping sauce

So utterly simple, this recipe is ideal for high summer when beans and peas in all their guises are cheap and plentiful, or indeed, as a way of using them up if you grow your own and have a glut. Gochugaru are Korean red pepper flakes and I'd urge you to seek them out – try an Asian grocery shop if you are lucky enough to have one nearby, or you can easily find them online. They add a slightly citrussy heat – intense but not hot – to this dipping sauce, which, incidentally, is delicious with pretty much anything that has an Asian twist.

**Serves 4–6**

Begin by making the dipping sauce – it will happily sit at room temperature for a couple of hours for the flavours to mingle, or for a day or so in the fridge. Put everything into a small bowl and whisk together, then pour into a serving bowl and set aside.

When you are ready to cook, fire up your barbecue, or preheat a large cast-iron griddle on the hob. Either way, you want your cooking surface to be really rather hot. When you think it's hot enough, flick on a few drops of water – they should sizzle and evaporate instantly.

The runner beans will take the longest to cook, so start with them. Put them into a bowl and add a little oil, just a teaspoon or so. Toss about until coated, then spread out on your super-hot grill, sprinkle with sea salt flakes and cook for about 3–4 minutes, until lightly charred, before turning and cooking on the other side. Transfer to a bowl and cover with a clean tea towel to keep warm. If your cooking surface is large, you may be able to cook everything at once. Otherwise, repeat in turn with the green beans, which will take 2–3 minutes, then the mangetout, which will cook the quickest.

Pile on to a large warmed plate, nestling the dish of gochugaru dipping sauce in the middle, and tuck in.

300g (10½oz) stringless runner beans
2 tsp vegetable oil
1 tsp sea salt flakes
300g (10½oz) fine green beans
300g (10½oz) mangetout (snow peas)

**For the gochugaru dipping sauce**
3 tbsp dark soy sauce
1 tbsp gochugaru (Korean red pepper flakes)
1 tbsp toasted sesame oil
1 tbsp toasted sesame seeds
1 tsp rice wine vinegar
1 tsp caster sugar
1 fat clove of garlic, crushed

# Caramelised fennel and oranges with whipped goat's cheese, butter beans and olives

Fennel and orange both grill particularly well, caramelising beautifully. I leave the skin on the orange slices so they retain some structural integrity on the grill, otherwise they have a tendency to shrivel up and disappear. The best way to eat them is to get stuck in with your fingers, nibbling the sticky sweet flesh off the rind as you go.

**Serves 4–6**

Fire up your barbecue ready for direct grilling, or preheat a griddle pan on the hob.

Begin by making the whipped goat's cheese, which is most easily done in a food processor or with an electric hand whisk. Failing that, a mixing bowl, wooden spoon and elbow grease will do the trick. Either way, you combine the cheese, cream, thyme leaves and orange zest to form a smooth, creamy paste, seasoning to taste with salt and pepper. Scoop into a bowl and set aside.

Drizzle a little olive oil on to the fennel wedges and orange slices, seasoning with salt and pepper. Lay them on the barbecue or griddle and cook until lightly charred and caramelised in places. Turn them over and move them around a few times to ensure they are cooking evenly. Depending on the heat, it will take about 15 minutes for the fennel and 10 minutes for the oranges. If the fennel is charred enough but not quite tender, move it further away from the heat or reduce the heat on the hob.

Meanwhile, tip the butter beans into a small fireproof pan or skillet and add the rest of the olive oil and the garlic. Season with salt and pepper and stir to mix, setting the pan on the barbecue to allow the beans to heat through. Or set over a medium heat on the hob if you are cooking inside.

When everything is cooked, tip the warmed beans on to a serving plate and top with the fennel and orange slices. Add little spoonfuls of the whipped goat's cheese on top and sprinkle over the olives. Finish with a few extra thyme leaves and the reserved orange zest and serve warm.

3 tbsp olive oil
about 500–600g (18–21oz) fennel (about 1 large bulb or 2–3 small), cut into 1cm (½ inch) wedges through the root
2 medium oranges, cut into 5mm (¼ inch) half-moon slices, skin left on
400g (14oz) can of butter beans, drained and rinsed
1 clove of garlic, crushed
a loose handful of black olives, roughly chopped
salt and freshly ground black pepper

**For the whipped goat's cheese**
250g (9oz) soft goat's cheese
75ml (¼ cup) double (heavy) cream
3–4 sprigs of thyme, leaves picked, plus a few extra to garnish
zest of 2 medium oranges (reserve some to garnish)

# Mechouia

Mechouia is a delicious spiced grilled vegetable salad from Tunisia that is dressed with hard-boiled eggs and olives to make a substantial summery dish. A plate of warm toasted pittas is all you need to serve alongside, but if you had time, the gozleme on page 132 would be lovely instead. Best cooked on a barbecue due to the long grilling time – the kitchen would get pretty smoky!

**Serves 4–6**

Fire up a barbecue ready for direct grilling. Add the whole tomatoes, chillies and peppers and cook until charred all over, turning regularly. Put them into a bowl and cover with clingfilm – this will loosen the skins ready for peeling. Put the garlic cloves on the grill and cook until soft and the skin is charred. Finally, add the onion wedges and cook until softening and lightly charred. When all the vegetables are cooked, allow them to cool enough so you can comfortably handle them.

Peel away and discard the tomato, chilli and red pepper skins, and deseed the peppers and chillies. Finely chop the flesh and place in a bowl. Squeeze the garlic cloves from the skins and mash the flesh on a chopping board with the flat of a knife, adding it to the bowl of vegetables. Discard the outer skin of the onions and the root and finely chop the flesh, also adding it to the bowl. Stir through the caraway and cumin seeds, pour in the olive oil and squeeze in the lemon juice. Add most of the parsley, reserving a little to garnish, and season with salt and pepper, gently stirring everything together. Scoop into a shallow serving dish – in an ideal world leave for an hour or two at room temperature for the flavours to mingle before serving.

Tuck the egg halves around the edge of the bowl of mechouia and scatter over the reserved parsley and the olives. Serve with warm pitta bread to tear up and dunk in.

10 large vine tomatoes
8 long green chillies
3 red (bell) peppers
1 bulb of garlic, whole and unpeeled
2 red onions, skins left on, cut into wedges through the root
3 tsp caraway seeds, toasted and ground
3 tsp cumin seeds, toasted and ground
75ml (¼ cup) extra virgin olive oil
juice of 1 lemon, to taste
a good handful of flat-leaf parsley, roughly chopped
salt and freshly ground black pepper

**To serve**

3 hard-boiled eggs, peeled and halved
a good handful of black olives, sliced
warm pitta bread

# Charred cabbage, chestnut, raisin and paprika butter

**I love grilled cabbage and here it gets doused in a rich, sweet, slightly spicy butter. This would make a fabulous side dish to a winter or, dare I say it, festive feast.**

**Serves 4–6 as a side dish**

Fire up your barbecue ready for direct grilling, or preheat a griddle pan on the hob.

Bring a large pan of lightly salted water to the boil and, once boiling, add the cabbage wedges. Blanch for just 2 minutes, then drain really well and put back into the pan. Drizzle in the oil and season with salt and pepper, tossing to mix.

Lay the cabbage wedges directly on the grill bars over the fire and cook for about 5 minutes each side, until lightly charred at the edges. Once charred, slide them away from the heat – you can pile them on top of each other, where they will keep warm and continue to soften a little while you make the sauce. If you are cooking inside on a griddle you may need to cook in batches unless your griddle is very large. In this case, keep the cooked wedges warm in a low oven while you cook the rest.

Once the wedges are cooked and being kept warm, set a flameproof frying pan directly over the fire, or on the hob over a medium-high heat if you are cooking inside. Add the chestnuts and allow to toast for about 5 minutes, depending on the heat you give them. Once they are a shade darker, add the butter, raisins, smoked paprika, cinnamon and a little salt and pepper, mixing together as the butter melts.

To serve, pile the cabbage on to warmed serving plates, or divide between several smaller plates if you prefer, and spoon over the sauce. Serve immediately while hot.

2 sweetheart cabbages, each cut
    into 8 slim wedges through the root
1 tbsp olive oil
180g (6oz) pack of pre-cooked
    chestnuts, roughly chopped
125g (4½oz) butter
50g (⅓ cup) raisins
1 heaped tsp smoked paprika
1 tsp ground cinnamon
salt and freshly ground black pepper

# Index

# Acknowledgements

A year spent taming an overgrown allotment into a productive plot has been the biggest inspiration in writing this book. Having the space to spread my gardening wings has been brilliant - there is nothing like a veg glut to trigger a bit of culinary experimentation! Huge thanks, then, have to go to my family, Rob, Izaac and Eve, for helping with the grunt work and for tolerating my new obsession.

My name might be on this cover but I am just a part of the equation here. Team Quadrille – thank you to all of you, I just love being one of your authors. Special thanks to Sarah for believing me when I said veg could conquer meat, and to Katherine, Emily and Claire for making the book look so beautiful, and to all of the publicity team for helping me shout about *Charred* to the world.

Thanks also to my agent Martine Carter for always being at the end of the phone.

Jason Ingram gets a massive thank you for the gorgeous photos and for being so stoical in the face of the sometimes truly dire weather on shoot days. Kate Clark from the Props Cupboard, thanks for being so generous with both your time and your wares. Thanks also to Steve from Flour and Ash in Bristol, who offered me his willing chefs' hands during a very busy shoot.

Martin and Lindsay at Napoleon Grills, thanks for loving my work. Sending the love right back, your barbecues are ace to cook on!

Finally, the biggest thanks has to go to the readers and cooks who buy my books and to the whole of the UK BBQ community, who are such a lovely, welcoming and supportive bunch.

**Publishing Director** Sarah Lavelle
**Copy Editor** Annie Lee
**Design Manager** Claire Rochford
**Designer** Katherine Keeble
**Cover Illustration** Ellie Foreman-Peck
**Photographer** Jason Ingram
**Food Styling** Genevieve Taylor
**Production Director** Vincent Smith
**Production Controller** Tom Moore

First published in 2019 by Quadrille, an imprint of Hardie Grant Publishing

Quadrille
52–54 Southwark Street
London SE1 1UN
quadrille.com

Text © Genevieve Taylor 2019
Photography © Jason Ingram 2019
Design and layout © Quadrille Publishing Limited 2019

Cataloguing in Publication Data: a catalogue record for this book is available from the British Library.

ISBN: 978 1 78713 427 0

Reprinted in 2019
10 9 8 7 6 5 4 3 2

Printed in China